8 CRAZY BELIEFS
THAT SCREW UP YOUR LIFE

Change These Beliefs and
Become a Healthier, Happier Person

Sharon S. Esonis, Ph.D.

8 Crazy Beliefs That Screw Up Your Life
Change These Beliefs and Become a Healthier, Happier Person

First printing 2012.

Esonis, Ph.D., Sharon S.
    8 Crazy beliefs that screw up your life. Change these beliefs and become a healthier, happier person.

    ISBN 978-0-9799497-3-9

Published by Positive Path Publishing.

ATTENTION CORPORATIONS, UNIVERSITIES, COLLEGES AND PROFESSIONAL ORGANIZATIONS. Quantity discounts are available on bulk purchases of this book for educational or gift purposes. Specialty books or book excerpts can also be created to fit specific needs. For information, please contact Sharon S. Esonis, Ph.D., via email at ThePositivePath@cox.net. Telephone: 760-746-PATH (7284). Website: www.PositivePathLifeCoaching.com.

Cover design by Amy Falco, www.FalcoCreative.net
Cover illustration: Hemera/Getty Images

This book is dedicated to the many clients and students with whom I've had the privilege to work who've dared to confront the "crazy beliefs" that held them back in life. Their commitment to change and tenacity to succeed have been heartwarming for me and, I hope, rewarding for them. I'm thankful to have been with them on part of their journey.

ABOUT THE AUTHOR

Sharon Esonis has spent the better part of three decades helping individuals live their dreams through her work as a licensed psychologist, life coach and author. An expert in human behavior and motivation, Dr. Esonis specializes in the burgeoning field of Positive Psychology, the scientific study of optimal human functioning and the core strengths that can lead to the achievement of one's personally-defined goals – what we call "the good life."

Dr. Esonis earned her Bachelor and Masters degrees at Ohio University and her doctoral degree at Boston College. While at BC, she studied under a preeminent psychologist who was renowned in the field of Cognitive Behavior Therapy and was an early proponent of the Positive Psychology movement.

Dr. Esonis is licensed in psychology in Arizona and Massachusetts, and in addition to her many years of private practice as a clinician and life coach, she supervised masters and doctoral students in their clinical work at Arizona State University. She has served as a hospital staff psychologist and has lectured on topics ranging from stress management, meditation and relaxation training to assertiveness and sleep management. Today, her private practice in San Diego is dedicated exclusively to Positive Psychology Coaching.

Her first book, *It's Your Little Red Wagon... 6 Core Strengths for Navigating Your Path to the Good Life* was Dr. Esonis' initial contribution to the field of Positive Psychology, presenting proven success factors and strength-building techniques that can lead individuals to a life of purpose, motivation and personally-defined happiness.

In *8 Crazy Beliefs That Screw Up Your Life. Change These Beliefs and Become a Healthier, Happier Person,* Dr. Esonis identifies eight "Thematic Belief Systems" that, in her experience as a psychologist and life coach for over 30 years, prevent individuals from building healthy, long-lasting relationships and extracting maximum happiness from life. She examines these "crazy beliefs" with all their negative implications and offers practical, persuasive arguments for why – and how – they can be replaced with healthy alternatives.

Dr. Esonis is a member of the Association for Behavior and Cognitive Therapy (ABCT), the San Diego Professionals Coaches Alliance (SDPCA) and is a Founding Member of the Centre for Applied Positive Psychology (CAPP).

TABLE OF CONTENTS

INTRODUCTION

"The doors we open and close each day decide the lives we live."
Flora Whittemore

Our beliefs about ourselves, others and the world we live in have a profound impact on the quality and control we have in our lives. Beliefs often develop without our knowledge or approval. Our perceptions and interpretations can become fixed entities to which we strongly attach and which we fiercely protect. Our beliefs evolve through many sources: what we've been taught; experiences we've had and our interpretations of those experiences; what we've learned to fear; and what significant people in our lives have modeled for us. Beliefs generally aggregate in what I call "Thematic Belief Systems," such as one's need to seek approval or to be perfect, with specific sub-beliefs that define the theme. This book is about eight Thematic Belief Systems that have come up again and again in my practice as a psychologist and in my classes with students. A number of colleagues report the same themes in their therapy practices.

By helping clients and students identify and change these debilitating beliefs, many individuals have found their own voice and have thus become healthier and happier. Because of the effectiveness of this approach, I decided to put these specific belief systems into writing and call them *crazy beliefs* -- since they foment nothing but trouble. Most people with these beliefs are not crazy in the clinical sense, but they're definitely not thinking straight, and the consequences they experience can be very upsetting and debilitating. Sometimes they may even think they're going crazy!

Marshall McLuhan, the Canadian educator, philosopher and scholar, maintains that "Most of our assumptions have outlived their usefulness." Unfortunately, people seldom take a hard look at their beliefs and weigh whether they are based in reality, serve them well or cause paralysis and distress. Thematic Belief Systems offer a framework for interpreting the events we experience. Since our beliefs play a large role in defining our reality, our decisions and our behavior, it behooves each of us to take stock of our thinking patterns frequently and thoughtfully. Keep in mind that the more

1

entrenched a belief becomes, the greater the difficulty in questioning or changing that belief. Interestingly, because infants do not yet possess the ability to formulate opinions and have the automatic awareness to comprehend and manipulate what goes on in the cognitive domain, they don't have emotional biases. Animals, as well, are free of these biases. Their actions are governed by evidence and reason alone – not opinions, interpretations or assumptions.

Our beliefs are often challenged when information comes our way that's antithetical to how we see things. When there's a discrepancy between what we have come to believe and the new information that contradicts these beliefs, we often experience a state of confusion and discomfort. This phenomenon is known in psychology as "cognitive dissonance." When this occurs, the human tendency is to relieve the discomfort by reaffirming the original belief. The approach is either to consider the ideas that support the current belief to be more credible or to focus on ideas that refute the new information. There is, however, a healthier choice: to be open to the new information and identify ways to accommodate it into the current belief system, or to be willing to change your belief entirely if that's indicated. In this way you update your beliefs so they become more realistic and empowering.

When we address our current beliefs, we should be asking questions such as:

Is there enough evidence to support this belief?
What limitations do I experience because of thinking this way?
How do these beliefs affect my relationships and functioning?

By asking ourselves these questions, we have the opportunity to decide if modifications to our thinking are in order. In *8 Crazy Beliefs That Screw Up Your Life! Change These Beliefs and Become a Healthier, Happier Person,* I offer specific criteria to investigate each of these belief systems so you can determine which ones are applicable and, as a result, learn effective strategies to help make the changes necessary for better health and happiness.

The French novelist and critic Marcel Proust tells us, "The real voyage of discovery consists not in seeing new landscapes but in having new eyes." Adopting reality-based, healthy beliefs is a smart place to start for those who are disappointed in their lives or who simply want to make some needed recalibrations. I encourage you to make the decision to identify, challenge and change beliefs that no longer work… I can promise you that you won't be sorry!

Chapter 1
AFRAID OF ADVERSITY?

"Mishaps are like knives that either serve us or cut us as we grasp
them by the blade or the handle."
James Russell Lowell

The ADVERSITY BELIEF:
Experiencing adversity is unfair, frightening and demoralizing

This belief is a problem if you tell yourself:

o Adversity is a bad thing--something to be feared and avoided
o Nothing good can come from misfortune
o My life should not have obstacles; it should be smooth and stress-
free
o I must worry about all the things that can go wrong
o I am unable to handle bad news; it makes me feel helpless and out
of control
o When things go wrong I need others to get me through
o When things are difficult, it affects my whole life
o When things are difficult I lose hope for the future
o When I make a mistake or fail at something it means that
something is wrong with me
o There is no way I can be happy if bad things happen to me
o Mistakes and failures are shameful
o Mistakes and failures mean I am not perfect and that is
unacceptable

There are many people who truly believe that their lives should be
free from mistakes, failures, traumas, crises, personal limitations,
obstacles and all prickly problems. They have the notion that when
adversity occurs, life isn't treating them fairly, or they interpret the
dilemma as indicative of some personal deficiency. They may think
they don't have nor will ever have what it takes to cope with
difficulties, so adversity takes on the persona of the boogie man.
This set of beliefs can be quite debilitating because the message is
that you are powerless. Where does one go from there? Nowhere.

Adversity touches every one of us. No exceptions. I remember long ago I met a young woman in her late 20's who had had an idyllic childhood, no problems, no trials and tribulations. Sounds great, right? Life hit her hard with the unexpected death of her brother who was just a few years older than she. She fell apart, really fell apart. Now I'll grant you that something that terrible would greatly affect any loving sister. But because she had never had to handle anything difficult, she was poorly prepared for a tragedy of this magnitude. She was probably poorly prepared for any major upheaval. She had not learned the skills to help her cope and bounce back. It's quite true that we do our children no favors by protecting them from many of the distressing circumstances that present important opportunities for them to learn how to be resilient. Childhood is about being in training to handle what comes later in life. Joyce Maynard points out, "Imagine if you succeeded in making the world perfect for your children what a shock the rest of life would be for them."

In our internal conversations we tell ourselves why things happen, who is to blame and what might happen in the future. The negative events that occur in your life are not nearly as important as what you tell yourself about the meaning and expected effects of those events. I'm going to say that again because this point is so important. *The things that happen to you are not nearly as important as what you tell yourself about those events.* Your interpretation is a strong determinant in how your future will play out and if you view yourself as powerful or helpless. Life has lots of ups and downs for all of us. One major factor that differentiates the person who is healthy, happy and prospering from someone who is struggling, overwhelmed, and feeling out of control is the understanding that disappointments, failures, challenges and yes, even tragedies, are facts of life, and that a person can learn to meet these difficulties with resolve and resilience. Theodore Rubin explains that, "The problem is not that there are problems. The problem is expecting otherwise and thinking that having a problem is a problem."

Mistakes: Don't allow mistakes to blunt your motivation and stop your forward momentum.

The famous Austrian psychiatrist, Alfred Adler, reminds us of how things really work: "What do you first do when you learn to swim? You make mistakes, do you not? And what happens? You make other mistakes, and when you have made all the mistakes you possibly can without drowning -- and some of them many times over -- what do you find; that you can swim? Well, life is just the same as learning to swim! Do not be afraid of making mistakes, for there is no other way of learning how to live!"

I continue to find it curious that so many people expect to achieve their goals and dreams without making mistakes. Mistakes are a huge part of the learning curve and are more times than not opportunities in disguise. Everyone makes them. What counts most is your view of how they impact the situation. If you interpret a mistake as a personal shortcoming or a sign that you're not going to succeed, it will likely result in the deflation of your confidence and a weakening of your resolve to keep moving forward toward your goal. It is important to normalize mistakes in your belief system. In his metaphor for life's journey, Abraham Lincoln tells us, "The path was worn and slippery. My foot slipped from under me, knocking the other out of the way... but I recovered and said to myself, 'It's a slip and not a fall.'"

Failures: Treat failure as just another step on the way to success.

Some people fear and avoid failure as if it is the ultimate catastrophe. They see it as a personal indictment of their abilities and character. They may believe that perfection is the major objective in life and failures and mistakes are black marks on their personal report card. This is really quite far from reality -- another case of having wacky expectations that have no basis in fact. It's important to recognize that it's not failure, but fear of failure, that impairs performance and delays success. The most impressive success stories are of those folks who failed again and again, but who did not let failures affect their persistence and motivation. They were flexible and adaptable. They beat the odds by expecting to eventually triumph and by continuing to do whatever was necessary to prevail. Daniel Amen, M.D., points out, "Most of us look at our successes in the same positive way. It's how we deal with our failures that determines what we get out of life." True failure occurs when you quit because you believe failure is an end point.

Many people treat failure and success as if they are absolutes. One either fails at something or succeeds. Again, this idea is outside the realm of how things really are. Failure and success are interactive and on a continuum. F. Scott Fitzgerald declared, "Never confuse a single defeat with a final defeat." Michael Jordan, the professional basketball superstar, admits to his mistakes and failures: "I have missed more than 9000 shots in my career. I have lost almost 300 games. On 26 occasions I have been entrusted to take the game winning shot…and missed. And I have failed over and over and over again in my life. And that is why… I succeed."

Disappointments

Robert Kiyosaki, author of *Rich Dad, Poor Dad,* tells us, "The size of your success is measured by the strength of your desire, the size of your dream, and how you handle disappointment along the way." There is an equation that I often present to my clients and students: **"Expectation minus reality = frustration."** When you expect things to be different than what reality dictates, you set yourself up for disappointment and frustration.

Your expectations may be of others, or of how the world should treat you, or both. This is a phenomenon I see again and again. Let's take the client who's surprised that her mother has once again divulged personal information to her friends that the client told her in the strictest confidence. She seems shocked and disappointed. As her therapist, I am definitely not surprised because the best predictor of future behavior is past behavior, and her mother has done this again and again. This client is not recognizing the reality of the situation and, thus, continues to be deeply disappointed and angry. She's got two choices in this equation: She can change her expectation and thereby be undaunted by her mother's violation of the confidence; or she can change the reality by not telling her mother any information she doesn't want passed on.

The thing about disappointment that one needs to understand is the importance of identifying the reality of the factors involved, deciding what can and cannot be changed and then refusing to take personally what is beyond his or her control. Eliza Tabor notes that, "Disappointment to a noble soul is what cold water is to burning metal; it strengthens, tempers, intensifies, but never destroys it."

Obstacles: View obstacles as normal and surmountable.

Frank A. Clark concludes, "If you find a path with no obstacles, it probably doesn't lead anywhere." Obstacles are to be expected; don't be afraid of them. They often present the opportunity to reevaluate your plan and recharge your battery. If you don't expect them, you will spend a lot of time being frustrated. If you do expect them, you will be way ahead of the game.

Walt Disney was a shining example of not letting obstacles and difficulties get in the way of his dreams. A nervous breakdown, many financial catastrophes and a long, arduous road to his goals could not deter him from his journey toward Mickey Mouse and Disneyland. He recalls, "He [Mickey Mouse] popped out of my head onto a drawing pad… on a train ride from Manhattan to Hollywood at a time when business fortunes of my brother Roy and myself were at lowest ebb, and disaster seemed right around the corner."

Disney further notes, "When we opened Disneyland, a lot of people got the impression that it was a get-rich-quick thing, but they didn't realize that behind Disneyland was the great organization that I built here at the studio, and they all got into it and we were doing it because we loved to do it." He concludes that, "All the adversity I've had in my life, all my troubles and obstacles, have strengthened me…. You may not realize it when it happens, but a good kick in the teeth may be the best thing in the world for you."

Limitations

A real challenge for many people involves a personal limitation. The attitude one develops about the physical, psychological, cognitive, financial and other impediments can make all the difference in the world in how gratifying and meaningful one's life is. As Hubert H. Humphrey declares, "Oh, my friend, it's not what they take away from you that counts. It's what you do with what you have left."

One of my favorite examples of someone with considerable physical challenges who demonstrated a resilient and remarkable attitude is Helen Keller. She was a masterful force in living a life of purpose and fulfillment in spite of her very challenging handicaps. She was born on June 27, 1880. At the age of 19 months she contracted "brain fever," now known as scarlet fever. She suffered a complete loss of her hearing and sight.

Against tremendous odds, Helen Keller achieved great accomplishments as an author, speaker and activist. She traveled throughout the world, campaigning for civil rights, women's rights, voting rights and world peace. She was a devoted advocate for the blind and handicapped. By viewing her limitations as opportunities to make the world a better place, Helen Keller was a shining example of attitude over circumstances. She notes, "I seldom think about my limitations and they never make me sad. Perhaps there is just a touch of yearning at times, but it is vague, like a breeze among flowers." She is an inspiration in telling us, "We could never learn to be brave and patient if there were only joy in this world;" that "character cannot be developed in ease and quiet. Only through experience of trial and suffering can the soul be strengthened, ambition inspired and success achieved."

Crises, tragedies, traumas: Know that this too will pass.

A Chinese proverb advises that, "You cannot prevent the birds of sorrow from flying over your head, but you can prevent them from building nests in your hair." The first step toward managing serious adversity is to understand and accept three important beliefs: one, bad things happen to everyone and very bad things happen to many people; two, we often have little or no control over the occurrence of traumatic events and serious problems; and three, we have a choice about how we perceive, react to and utilize these events.

Understanding and accepting these realities is an important step on the path to becoming resilient. People who are resilient have developed skills that help them bounce back in tough times. They have beliefs and behaviors that are adaptable and proactive. Those without the skills are often at the mercy of life's crises and are susceptible to responses of anguish and despair that can last a very long time. Fortunately for them, these skills can be learned. A key part of a belief system that will help you in terrible times is accepting that life's major difficulties are surmountable and that the future, even in the midst of heavy black clouds, holds the promise of sunshine and renewal. As Friedrich Nietzsche's famous quote declares, "That which does not kill us makes us stronger."

Even though it may seem hard to believe, traumas, catastrophes and crises often are followed by special happenings. Take the example of the parent who loses a child in a drunk driving accident and makes it her life mission to bring the subject to the public's attention in order to prevent similar accidents from happening. This is dedication and passion rising out of disaster. Robert Brault posits, "Sometimes in tragedy we find our life's purpose -- the eye sheds a tear to find its focus." Finding purpose in tragedy can be a very resilient response that helps one move forward.

Bad things that might happen: Avoid obsessing about all that can go wrong.

"Catastrophizing" or "awfulizing," as we say in psychology, is a depressing, slippery slope that traps one in a preoccupation about all the things that can go wrong in the near or distant future. It can become a brain lock – pervasive and overwhelming. You have to be careful, for as Isaac Bashevis Singer, the Nobel Laureate in Literature, admonishes us, "If you keep on saying things are going to be bad, you have a good chance of becoming a prophet." Some people actually believe that by thinking about the worst possible scenarios they become less likely to experience them. Now that is truly superstitious behavior!

Sometimes catastrophizing is the result of having experienced one or more overwhelming difficulties that have left a person feeling helpless. Or maybe the catastrophizer had a parent or significant person in her childhood who was very afraid and passed it on. Or maybe an anxiety disorder predisposes an individual to think about the worst that can happen. Being inundated by bad news from all over the world because of the 24-hour news availability also plays a role in keeping danger on people's minds incessantly. But no matter how you got to this point, it's a very stressful way to live and diminishes your ability to cope with the difficulties that actually do occur. You might want to think about Rodney Dangerfield's wisecrack, "My wife was afraid of the dark... then she saw me naked and now she's afraid of the light." With the catastrophizer, it's always something! When one fear fades from focus, some other fear replaces and dominates her internal world. This is a pretty lousy way to live. Identify any instances of catastrophizing in your life. Utilize two techniques that can be found in the last chapter: Disputing and the Self-Control Triad can help get this under control.

An optimistic attitude serves you well in tough times

Developing an optimistic attitude is a powerful way to navigate troubled waters and to increase the opportunities and successes in your life. Optimism is a belief system. Optimists have the belief in their own power to make life and the future better, and they typically have the belief that negative events **are not** permanent, personal or pervasive. Let me explain what that means.

Permanent refers to the lasting effects of an event. If you make a mistake, fail at some task, encounter an obstacle, face a crisis or suffer a heart wrenching loss, do you tell yourself that this is not going to go away or change, that this problem is permanent? Or do you, as the optimist, tell yourself that this is a temporary state of affairs and that things will get better with time and effort? An example of permanent is the belief that because you lost a job that future jobs will end that way as well.

Personal refers to your interpretation of who or what is responsible for the event and why it happened. If you're besieged by a negative event, do you believe you're a victim or that you brought this terrible thing upon yourself? Or, as the optimist, do you believe bad things happen to everyone, that your response to them is what will make the difference in the future? An example of personal is the belief that because the boss criticized the project you've been working on, she doesn't like you and no matter what you do she'll find fault with it.

Pervasive pertains to your belief about how other parts of your life will be affected by the event. In the case of a negative event, do you believe this will have a counterproductive influence on other aspects of your life, or as the optimist, believe that the effect is specific to the context in which it occurred? An example of pervasive: You have a problem with your boss at work. Do you let this difficulty infiltrate your time with your family and friends? Does it spoil your golf game on the weekend?

Optimism is about knowing you are responsible for your life and that you have the ability to be effective on your own behalf. People who are optimistic have a more positive inner world, are happier, and have healthier relationships. They develop more productive behaviors and abilities, which often lead to the successful completion of goals and the realization of dreams.

Optimism is not about being "Susie Sunshine" or a Pollyanna. Optimism is about getting it, understanding that bad and good things happen to everyone. President Harry Truman makes a wonderful distinction about optimists and pessimists: "The pessimist is one who makes difficulties of his opportunities, and an optimist is one who makes opportunities of his difficulties."

What about the frightening feelings and scary thoughts that are a normal part of really tough situations? Do optimists experience them? Yes, indeed. Susan Vaughan, the psychiatrist who authored *Half Empty, Half Full,* explains that the optimist is one who knows she can handle whatever is thrown her way. She can tolerate negative feelings because of her belief in her ability to bounce back. She understands that it is okay to feel bad. So even in the midst of difficulty and emotional turmoil, she will formulate a plan for moving forward.

It's important to remember that it's your choice where you focus your attention. You may want to learn some specific techniques that reinforce your control, such as thought stopping and disputing. These techniques can be quite effective if you decide you want to take greater command. More information on these techniques is contained in Chapter 9.

Chapter 2
ADDICTED TO APPROVAL?

"None of us will ever accomplish anything excellent or commanding except when he listens to this whisper which is heard by him alone."
Ralph Waldo Emerson

The APPROVAL BELIEF: I need the approval of others to feel good about myself and to feel safe.

This belief is a problem if you tell yourself:

o I should not disappoint others
o Being approved of is the most important thing in life
o If I don't do what others want me to do, I will lose their respect and love
o If people don't approve of me, there must be something wrong with me
o I must avoid conflict with others or they will not like me
o I shouldn't make decisions that might offend someone
o I need others to help me make decisions
o My happiness depends on others
o I know people are often evaluating me
o Criticism means I am not measuring up
o It's important for me to apologize when someone is hurt so that person will feel better
o I should feel bad if I've disappointed someone
o If I do many nice things for people they will approve of me and like me
o How others see me is how I really am
o I believe others have the right to judge me
o I am a good person if I pay more attention to the needs of others than I do to my own
o It's important for me to forgive people even if I don't feel like it
o I should critique myself often, finding what others might find objectionable about me

There's a rarely discussed addiction that can be as enslaving as drugs and as devastating to self-respect, self-confidence and healthy functioning as alcoholism. The obsessive need for approval brings with it a lot of baggage! It promotes failure and disappointment, wastes time and energy, and fosters dependence, anxiety, depression and exhaustion. If this is your drug of choice, you can expect a life where you are trapped in the stress zone.

In this type of existence you are not the architect of your own life. Rachel Naomi Remen, physician and early pioneer in the mind/body field, asserts, "To seek approval is to have no resting place, no sanctuary. Like all judgment, approval encourages a constant striving. It makes us uncertain of who we are and of our true value. Approval cannot be trusted. It can be withdrawn at any time no matter what our track record has been. It is as nourishing of real growth as cotton candy. Yet many of us spend our lives pursuing it."

When you care too much about the acceptance and applause of others you give your power away. Just as the junkie who craves drugs is controlled by dependence on the substances, the approval addict who craves validation and appreciation is dependent on the whims of other people. Trouble for sure. Dependence is a slippery slope. You find yourself relying on others, hoping they will treat you with the same kindness and consideration they wish for themselves. Dependency enslaves you, giving others the ultimate power over how you perceive and feel about yourself. Do you really want to surrender something so personally vital?

This is dangerous territory. People often have their own agendas and prejudices that may serve neither to assuage your fears nor promote your best interests. Or they may tell you the truth, something you probably don't want to hear if you're struggling with this particular affliction. The truth might crush you because you seek only approval and are wholly unprepared for anything else. You may believe you are unable to be okay when the feedback you receive is critical or disapproving. But worst of all, by not being your own primary source of approval, by depending on others for what you should be providing for yourself, you make it supremely difficult to be healthy, happy and prosperous. As Claudius Claudianus tells us, "The person who seeks all their applause from outside has their happiness in another's keeping."

According to Karen Revich, Ph.D. and Andrew Shatte in *The Resilience Factor,* people who need approval tend to be over-reactive to the negative responses and conflicts that come up for all of us in life. They often over-interpret the behavior of others, mind read and take personally what happens, even when the responses may have little or nothing to do with them.

How Does This Happen?

Just how does this ineffectual, paralyzing approach become a way of life? If you're caught in the approval trap, there's a very good chance that you developed this as a result of messages from significant people in your formative years. They may have reinforced you for seeking approval, or they may have criticized you unduly or inappropriately, resulting in feelings of fear, helplessness and inadequacy. Or they may have lived *their* lives in the approval trap, thus modeling the behaviors and the thinking that are inherent in this particular dysfunctional pattern.

Sometimes parents, often unwittingly, reinforce approval-seeking behaviors beyond what is healthy. Why would they do this? Well, it can be very rewarding for them. They look like great parents because the child is so compliant. They find the child's interactions to be very pleasing. And the parenting job is so easy with a child like this! The child, however, is learning to wear the shackles of the approval trap, often interpreting what is occurring as a successful way to approach life both within and outside the family.

Perhaps your parents or other important people in your life expected too much. And when you weren't able to meet those expectations you were criticized and ridiculed. When individuals are subjected to a steady diet of criticism, especially as children, they become fearful of being criticized, so they may put inordinate amounts of energy into findings ways to avoid the slings and arrows. To escape criticism, the child may hide from the source or may direct the lion's share of his energy to garnering approval and applause. This approach is so exhausting.

Children also can learn to make approval-seeking a way of life when they see these behaviors modeled by important people in their lives. When parents, older siblings and other significant people in a child or adolescent's life are approval junkies, youngsters often conform to the behaviors, expectations and thinking processes of those they love, need, admire or fear.

In many cultures, religions and communities, females are taught to seek the approval by focusing their efforts on taking care of others -- often to the exclusion of self-care and self-responsibility. Because this expectation is pervasive, its identification and insidiousness often go unrecognized by the individual.

In psychology we often talk about external versus internal locus of control. The approval addict is governed almost entirely by external locus of control -- that is, she is ruled by the responses of other people and by the circumstances that occur. She has a reactive approach and thus very little control over her life. People who are in command of their own lives have a healthy level of internal locus of control. They are proactive, not reactive. Let me note here that individuals can also have too great a degree of internal locus of control when they have no regard for the opinions and needs of others.

The Benefits of Getting Out of the Approval Trap

According to Tehyi Hsieh, "Lean too much on the approval of other people, and it becomes a bed of thorns." You have much to look forward to when you emancipate yourself from this unhealthy addiction. And though it may take some time and a heap of persistence, if you choose this route you are going to like yourself and your life so much more! Of course, the path may initially evoke some fear and discomfort, but if taken step by step, it will get manageable and then exhilarating.

When you work to get out of the approval trap you'll find yourself feeling more independent and self-reliant. You choose for yourself. You become your own cheerleader. You decide what things matter and what things don't. People are far less likely to be able to take advantage of you when you are the primary source of your own approval. You no longer believe that others have a right to judge you. You believe that the control of your life comes from an internal place and not from external circumstances and the responses of others. You believe you have the right and the responsibility to decide how the behavior and opinions of others will affect you. Mahatma Gandhi explains, "The only tyrant I will accept in this world is the still, small voice within me."

Your self-confidence and self-respect will soar as you become more your own person. Self-confidence and self-respect come from believing in your abilities and taking responsibility for your own life. You accept yourself, warts and all. You are able to free yourself from the expectations of others, opening up so many ways to get to know and respect yourself.

You become capable of developing healthier and more robust relationships. When you're not ensnared in the approval trap, you're far better able to develop the fundamental building blocks of flourishing personal relationships: trust, mutual respect, self-respect, appropriate boundaries and a balance of power. According to Honore De Balzac, "Nothing is a greater impediment to being on good terms with others than being ill at ease with yourself."

Your ability to problem-solve and reach your goals gets a big boost. When the approval of others takes a back seat, you are able to face the challenges in your life from a position of power. Of course, it's often wise to consult with specific people about problems and goals, but this is a far cry from depending on others to dictate what you ought to do. You understand that your decisions, beliefs and behaviors are powerful in determining the outcomes in your life.

With your liberation from this addiction you will become better able to tolerate conflict and rejection. Because you don't consider others to be your ultimate judges and because you believe others have their own issues, you're able to respond to conflict and rejection in more adaptive ways. And with each conflict or rejection, you learn you can become stronger. Keep in mind that "Peace is not the absence of conflict, but the ability to cope with it." (Author Unknown)

When you think and decide for yourself you become less susceptible to the learned helplessness that so often factors into depression and anxiety. Learned helplessness is the state in which you believe your actions do not affect what happens in your life. The person dependent on the opinions of others is so often beset by this belief. Your own self-approval is contingent on the approval of one or more persons in your world. When you take control of your own world you become more immune to being anxious and depressed.

The Way Out of the Trap: You need to replace old, ineffectual beliefs with healthy ones that reinforce your authority over your own life.

Okay, so you're up to your neck in the sludge of the approval trap. Please don't despair. Instead, let me encourage you, no matter how long you've been stuck in the mud or how deeply you're submerged, to make the changes that will set you free and keep you from returning to your own personal hell. To accomplish your emancipation from the trap, you'll need to develop approval-free beliefs, expectations and self-talk. The techniques of disputing and thought stopping can be very helpful in this endeavor. A discussion of these techniques can be found in the last chapter of this book. The person with approval issues might also be helped by learning the principles of assertiveness. Two very informative books on this subject are *Your Perfect Right* by Alberti and Emmons, and *The Assertive Woman* by Phelps and Austin.

Healthy beliefs include:

Your happiness is something only you can make happen

In her excellent book, *The How of Happiness* (2007), Sonja Lyubomirsky of the University of California at Riverside reveals that up to 40% of our happiness is within our power to change. Forty percent! And one of the real eye openers is the relative unimportance of "life circumstances" in determining how happy people are. That's right all those things -- either positive or negative -- that happen to individuals affect only 10% of their happiness quotient. Many people erroneously believe that external variables are the most important determinants of well-being. But Lyubomirsky has found that what really contributes to happiness are the individual's intentional activities. She tells us, "In a nutshell, the fountain of happiness can be found in how you behave, what you think, and what goals you set everyday of your life. Happiness is more achievable when you command your own ship." As broadcaster and author Hugh Downs asserts, "A happy person is not a person in a certain set of circumstances, but rather a person with a certain set of attitudes."

The judgment of others does not have to be how you see yourself. Just because others tell you that you are inept, lazy, stupid, a failure, a disappointment, etc. does not mean it's true

Eleanor Roosevelt contends, "No one can make you feel inferior without your consent." Why would you automatically believe such mean-spirited and harmful declarations from others? When others deliver insults such as these, do you believe they have your best interests at heart? Or is it more likely that this is a form of manipulation? It makes more sense for you to evaluate your own behavior and its consequences. If you need more input, ask for feedback from people you trust and who you feel care about you -- and who have no "skin in the game." Constructive criticism can be helpful. Constructive criticism is compassionate, useful and intended to assist you. For those who attack you with disparaging labels, remember what W.C. Fields maintains: "It ain't what they call you, it's what you answer to."

Disappointing others is not a catastrophe

People often have expectations of you that are unreasonable and out of bounds. They may feel entitled to their expectations even if their conclusions are way off the mark. When someone expresses disappointment in you, it's a good idea to examine objectively the appropriateness of their expectations. To just assume that another has the unconditional right to be disappointed with you gives them too much power over your life. Again, the person most responsible for setting personal expectations is you. Remember the wise words of Anatole France: "If a million people say a foolish thing, it is still a foolish thing."

The approval that is most important is your own

When you accept that you're in command of your own path in life, you conclude that you don't need the approval of others. Is it gratifying to have the approval of others? Sure, but understanding that it's not necessary for your happiness, success and mental health is key. The Greek stoic philosopher Epictetus maintains, "God has entrusted me with myself." It really is quite liberating to know that you have the right and the ability to be CEO of your own life. As CEO, remember to be generous with your approval and to abstain from being perfectionistic.

Chapter 3
DEPENDENT UPON OTHERS?

"There came a time when the risk to remain tight in the bud was more painful than the risk it took to blossom."
Anais Nin

The DEPENDENCY BELIEF: I need or want to depend on others.

This belief is a problem if you tell yourself:

o I'm not as brave and capable as other people
o Something bad will happen if I have no one on whom to depend
o I wouldn't know what to do if I were on my own
o I don't want to give up the comfort of being taken care of by others
o Why shouldn't someone take care of me? I deserve it
o Parents are supposed to take care of their kids no matter how old they are
o Others like to do things for me, it makes them happy so what's wrong with that?
o It's okay to take money and gifts from others, to have people support me
o Without a partner I would be so lonely and lost
o Relationships will solve my problems and make me happy
o Not having a partner is catastrophic
o You're supposed to be dependent on your partner
o Women need to have someone on whom to rely
o Men need someone on whom to rely

Human beings thrive when they have close and interdependent relationships. On one hand, these relationships are about being your own person, and on the other hand, being connected in healthy ways to others. Dependency is a very different matter. When individuals rely on others to do for them what they can and should do for themselves, they shift the control of their lives to other people. This makes it difficult for them to develop their own identity and to fulfill their own potential. Tommy Lasorda, the baseball Hall of Fame manager, explains in his sports metaphor about life: "There are three types of baseball players -- those who make it happen, those who watch it happen, and those who wonder what happened." Dependent people regrettably find themselves again and again in the last two groups.

The dependent person becomes enslaved by needs and fears. In many areas she becomes unable to take the risks that lead to life's successes and rewards. With dependency, fears grow and self-confidence shrinks day by day. A person's locus of control -- who or what manages an individual's life -- comes from outside. The dependent person's life is really not her own. She has relinquished her power to others, which so often impedes her chances of being genuinely happy. As William Arthur Ward warns us, "Happiness is an inside job."

Another type of dependent person is the individual who isn't so much afraid as she is quite content having others take care of things so she can be comfortable and satisfied with little effort. She prefers not having to push herself too hard or make the sacrifices it takes to maintain the status quo, let alone go beyond. She is often dependent on the caretaker-type person whose identity revolves around being needed by others. On the surface this may appear to be beneficial for both, but it's a relationship without authenticity, integrity or growth. An Irish proverb declares, "You've got to do your own growing, no matter how tall your grandfather is."

Whether due to fear, indolence or entitlement, expecting others to take care of you is a recipe for disaster. By abdicating your responsibility for yourself, you've increased the likelihood of disappointment, resentment and complicated, unhealthy relationships. Your beliefs and choices make it very hard for you to feel good about your life. You may wonder why you're so different from others. Instead of feeling safer you feel less safe and less secure. Your friends may continue to grow and thrive, leaving you behind, lonely and lost. J.W. Jepson maintains, "Real adulthood is the result of two qualities: self-discipline and self-reliance. The process of developing them together in balance is called maturing." The dependent individual is stalled, stuck and certainly not maturing and flourishing.

You're skating on thin ice if you expect any relationship, romantic or otherwise, to resolve your problems or fill the voids in your life. There may be times that you resent the person or people who do so much for you -- way too much! You may become obsessed with the possibility that someone will abandon you by death or by choice. You become focused on the ways to keep the other person in this codependent alliance. Feelings of helplessness prevail. You manipulate the other person so that the relationship will not change. Heaven forbid! You feel they must continue to take care of you. Thomas Szasz believes, "The proverb warns that 'You should not bite the hand that feeds you.' But maybe you should, if it prevents you from feeding yourself."

Resentment often abounds in situations where someone, usually due to fear or anxiety, relinquishes personal control. Even though you might hand it over willingly or gratefully, negatives feelings often arise when: 1) the other person expects you to do what's been advised and you don't like the recommendation; 2) the other person doesn't want the responsibility; or 3) heaven forbid, the person doesn't have your best interests at heart and gives you bum advice. Take for example the boyfriend, girlfriend, husband or wife who wants to control you and will use any means to make this happen, including emotional and/or physical abuse. T.S. Eliot warns, "If you haven't the strength to impose your own terms on life, you must accept the terms it offers you."

Let's talk about romantic dependency. Some people actually believe that not having a partner is the biggest catastrophe on earth, that there is only one way to live, one way to be healthy and happy, and that's to be part of a couple. This places inordinate pressure on what the "relationship" is expected to do for your life. When you expect your partner to make you happy, help you with all your decisions and fill your time, you're expecting way too much. The research is very clear on this topic. Happiness is something only you can make happen for yourself. Many of the clients I've seen over the years have found themselves bewildered by the effects of this mindset. And they were continually surprised by how poorly they were served by this reliance on "the relationship." Elizabeth Kubler-Ross contends that people are like stained glass windows: "They sparkle and shine when the sun is out, but when the darkness sets in their true beauty is revealed only if there is light within."

Others are ill-equipped to provide what would truly enhance the robustness of your life, because only you can do that. It's vital to trust yourself in making your life the way you want it to be. If you rely on others to convince you that you're special, worthy and accomplished, your self-esteem is at their mercy. And even if someone deeply loves you, this is far too much power to cede to them.

What can you expect from a life of dependency? Depression is often about feelings of helplessness, which go with the territory of being dependent, so there's a distinct possibility that you will suffer from a mood disorder or some level of depression. Anxiety is also quite common among those who continue to be dependent. With the resentment that often results from this approach to life, one may become beset by anger or rage. Let's just say the dependent person is hardly ever a "happy camper." James Thurber tells us:

All men should strive
to learn before they die
what they are running from, and to, and why.

When does dependence become a serious mental health issue?

When dependence is pervasive and debilitating, a diagnosis of Dependent Personality Disorder may be applicable. The National Institutes of Health defines personality disorders as "long-term patterns of thoughts and behaviors that cause serious problems with relationships and work. People with personality disorders have difficulty dealing with everyday stresses and problems. They often have stormy relationships with other people. The exact cause of personality disorders is unknown. However, genes and childhood experiences may play a role."

According to the Cleveland Clinic, the symptoms of Dependent Personality Disorder (DPD) are as follows: "People with DPD become emotionally dependent on other people and spend great effort trying to please others. People with DPD tend to display needy, passive, and clinging behavior, and have a fear of separation." Other common characteristics of this personality disorder include the following:

o Inability to make decisions, even everyday decisions, without the advice and reassurance of others
o Avoidance of personal responsibility; avoidance of jobs that require independent functioning and positions of responsibility
o Intense fear of abandonment and a sense of devastation or helplessness when relationships end; they often move right into another relationship when one ends
o Over-sensitivity to criticism
o Pessimism and lack of self-confidence, including a belief that they are unable to care for themselves
o Avoidance of disagreeing with others for fear of losing support or approval
o Inability to start projects
o Difficulty being alone
o Willingness to tolerate mistreatment and abuse from others
o Placing the needs of their caregivers above their own
o Tendency to be naïve and to live in fantasy

How does one become dependent?

As in the development of many personality characteristics, nature often factors into the equation. For example, a child who manifests anxiety is often more prone to depending on a "safe" person or persons. The child may have social anxiety, generalized anxiety, a phobia, obsessive-compulsive disorder or panic disorder. Anxiety may feed one's lack of self-confidence, so the individual, being unsure of herself, feels compelled to rely on another in many ways.

Children who are reared by an overprotective, caretaking parent may become dependent on that parent. The overprotection delivers the message that the child is not capable of handling life's twists and turns. This type of parenting style also makes it easy to avoid any situation that might involve discomfort and require problem-solving and resilience. Thus, the youngster doesn't get to experience the steppingstones to self-reliance. The overprotective parent and the dependent child have very murky boundaries. It's difficult for the child to know where she ends and the other person begins. If this pattern of dependence continues into adulthood, the individual can become quite handicapped in engineering a healthy and happy life for herself. Abraham Lincoln asserts, "The worst thing you can do for those you love is the thing they could and should do for themselves."

Authoritarian parenting may also lead to dependency. When it's difficult to feel safe or please a parent, the child can become manifestly unsure of herself. With the feelings of inadequacy that result, she looks for someone on whom to depend. Children who have been abused and/or neglected are at increased risk of becoming dependent. Their world is anything but predictable and safe. So they will find any "port in a storm."

Children can become socially behind when developmental milestones are not met in a timely fashion. Social deficits often make it hard to interact with peers; some children are bullied and made fun of, leading to dependency on a safe person such as a parent or relative. Children who have other challenges such as obesity, speech problems, hearing problems, etc., may also experience reactions from others that create discomfort and shame -- which can render an individual vulnerable to dependency.

ACHIEVING A LIFE OF BALANCE AND INDEPENDENCE

If you decide that you're overly dependent on the opinions of others and that you'd like to tackle this problem, congratulations! You have a lot to look forward to. There are many things you can do on your own to foster independence. If you find the going too tough, however, I would recommend that you talk to a professional who can help you face your fears. In a step-by-step manner you can learn to make your own decisions and design your own life. This work will involve setting and maintaining boundaries and learning to be assertive. Like any other dependency, it will take some time and effort, but it can be done and it is so worth it. Keep in mind the

27

Swedish proverb: "The best place to find a helping hand is at the end of your arm."

First, identify what beliefs and behaviors make you dependent

Spend some time identifying your dependency beliefs and behaviors. Also, determine what scares you about becoming more independent and/or why you haven't been motivated to escape the dependency trap. It might be helpful to check back to the first part of this article "This belief is a problem if you tell yourself..." Keep a notebook with the beliefs you identify. Add to your list as you think about this day to day. Then do the same with the dependent behaviors. If you continue to evaluate these factors for a week or so, you'll probably have discovered most of the important factors.

Develop the beliefs that promote self-reliance

The beliefs you discovered in your assessment need to be changed to proactive, self-reliant statements. When you tell yourself some of the old, dependent, self-defeating beliefs, be ready to replace them with statements that foster independence. Below are some examples. However, you may come up with many others that are more powerful for you.

o I am capable of making my life and future better
o The approval that is most important to me is my own
o I can handle and learn from criticism
o It is not a catastrophe to make a mistake or fail at something
o If I make a bad decision, it's not the end of the world
o I do not have to have a partner to live a happy life
o When I have a partner I still want to make my personal decisions
o I don't have to be afraid because I can take care of myself
o I believe independence is an important quality in my life
o I am the only one who can make my life the way I want it to be
o My life will be so much better if I take back my power

Developing behaviors that promote self-reliance

Behavior change takes time, effort and tenacity. This is often best done in steps that are small enough not to be overwhelming and large enough to give you some satisfaction and hope. Below is a list of behaviors that will help move you forward:

o Ask others for help only when you really need it
o Make your own decisions
o Face your fears
o Set goals that when met will encourage you and make you proud of yourself
o Choose your partner wisely, assessing if this person will respect and support your individuality and independence
o Refuse to let obstacles, mistakes, failures to get in the way of your forward progress
o Learn assertiveness
o Set appropriate boundaries with others and be sure to communicate what they are and enforce them
o Spend time dreaming of the future you want and then set your goals and path accordingly
o Experiment with new activities and situations that offer possibilities for growth and enjoyment
o Wean yourself off any financial dependence

Recommended readings

The Assertive Woman (2002) Phelps and Austin
Your Perfect Right (1995) Alberti and Emmons

References

Cleveland Clinic website:
http://my.clevelandclinic.org/disorders/personality_disorders/hic_de
pendent_personality_disorder.aspx

National Institutes of Health website:
http://www.nlm.nih.gov/medlineplus/personalitydisorders.html

Chapter 4
PLAGUED WITH UNREALISTIC EXPECTATIONS?

"Serenity comes when you trade expectations for acceptance."
Author Unknown

The EXPECTATION BELIEF: People should be the way I want them to be; my life should be the way I want it to be.

This belief is a problem if you tell yourself:

o People should believe what I believe
o Others should behave the way I want them to
o My friends and family should have the same emotional reactions to circumstances as I do
o People should follow the rules I consider important
o People close to me, especially my partner, should be willing to change to make me happy
o I should be upset when things are not the way I want them to be
o It's unfair when I expect something and it doesn't happen
o It's unfair and wrong when things happen that I believe should not

There is a hidden source of power or pain that often goes unaddressed by many individuals. The truth is, expectations can have a far-reaching impact on how people live their lives and the rewards and successes they reap along the way. Expectations are assumptions about the future – what will occur or what should occur – and they can profoundly influence your relationships, your self-confidence, your happiness and your ability to navigate your path in life.

What a huge mistake it is to ignore, deny or simply cling to expectations that have little or nothing to do with how things really work. Expecting too little or too much, or expecting inappropriate things of ourselves, other people in our lives and the world in which we live, can cause utter chaos. Paul Broca, the French physician and anthropologist, contends, "The least questioned assumptions are often the most questionable."

Unrealistic expectations can set you up for disappointment, ineffective behavior and even depression. **Expectation minus reality = frustration.** Our self-talk, moods and feelings are often governed by the frustration that results when what we expected would or should happen does not happen. Unexpected outcomes can seriously undermine a person's motivation and zest for life.

Relationships are profoundly affected by expectations. Unfortunately, some people – I would go as far as saying many people – don't give much consideration to what they're expecting from others and how these expectations may be affecting the health of their personal interactions. The Talmud tells us, "We do not see things as they are. We see them as we are." Our perceptions, opinions and beliefs often go unchallenged, as if they're unassailable because they're so much a part of who we are.

By choosing carefully, your expectations can lead to powerful plans and behavior. The actor Alan Alda suggests, "Begin challenging your own assumptions. Your assumptions are your windows on the world. Scrub them off every once in a while, or the light won't come in." Changing your expectations to those that are smart and adaptable will serve you well and is not as difficult as you might imagine. Doing so involves paying particular attention to reality and possibility, flexibly negotiating the two again and again.

EXPECTATION DON'TS

Don't expect others to think like you and believe what you believe

The 19th century German philosopher Friedrich Nietzsche sums up how things really are: "You have your way, I have my way. As for the right way, the correct way and the only way, it does not exist." There is a real danger in assuming that others are wrong because their experiences and views differ from yours. When this prejudicial assumption prevails, the believer may take on an air of superiority that's a hindrance to active listening, the resolution of conflicts and the development of close, mutually advantageous relationships. E. B. White, the American author, humorist and poet, contends, "Prejudice is a great time saver. You can form opinions without having to get the facts."

Do you tell yourself that you must continually prove that your opinions are correct and that being wrong is unacceptable? Do you think this approach of needing to be right is a sign of strength? If you answer these two questions in the affirmative, I wouldn't be a bit surprised if you're experiencing relationship difficulties. In *The Mastery of Love: A Practical Guide to the Art of Relationship*, Don Miguel Ruiz explains, "We learn to be right and to make everyone else wrong. The need to be right is the result of trying to protect the image we want to project to the outside. We have to impose our way of thinking, not just onto other humans, but even upon ourselves."

Keep in mind that listening and respecting the opinions of others does not necessarily mean you agree, but that you recognize and support the other person's right to think for himself. It may indicate that you want more information so you can learn and grow. Relationships function so much better when the opinions of each party are heard and respected.

Don't expect others to behave like you, have the same emotional reactions or follow your rules

Where in the world do some folks come up with the bizarre notion that they get to decide what constitutes appropriate, acceptable behavior? What's with the crazy idea that others should be like them, behave like them and want what they want? This mindset resides way outside of reality. People are different – and thank goodness for that! If you're deluded by this narcissistic attitude, your relationships would be far better served if you summarily dismissed this nonsense from your repertoire! It can be quite a relief to resign from the self-anointed position of grand rule legislator for the universe.

According to author and therapist James Krebiel, "Invariably, unrealistic expectations are connected to issues of power, manipulation and control. We might embrace an underlying assumption which says, 'People must act the way I want them to, or else I have no use for them.' Another twist on this theme is filled with rage and anger. It goes, 'People better act the way I want them to, or else I will pay them back!' Many times these assumptions are behind patterns of physical and emotional abuse. One partner will try to manipulate and control the behavior of their mate in order to get what they want. If the abused partner refuses, conflict ensues."

People who fear other individuals who behave differently or follow a different drummer live in a closed, threatening world of anger and frustration. The eminent cognitive behavioral psychologist, Albert Ellis, poses an important question: "Where is it written that others must act the way we want them to? It may be preferable but not necessary." I would add to that: Get your expectations in line with reality. Stop "shoulding" on those with whom you come in contact, especially the people who mean the most to you.

Leo F. Buscalia, the *New York Times* bestselling author of *Living, Loving Learning*, suggests, "A loving relationship is one in which the loved one is free to be himself -- to laugh with me but never at me; to cry with me but never because of me; to love life, to love himself, to love being loved. Such a relationship is based upon freedom and can never grow in a jealous heart." You have the power to significantly improve your relationships by working to maintain a balance of power. Each partner needs to have a sense of personal authority, significance and equality. Each needs the freedom to pursue his or her own personal goals in addition to the shared goals. H. Jackson Browne, the *New York Times* bestselling author of *Life's Little Instruction Book*, gets it exactly right when he points out, "People take different roads seeking fulfillment and happiness. Just because they're not on your road doesn't mean they've gotten lost."

Don't expect people to change for you

Oh my, do I see this phenomenon far too often, particularly in loving relationships! One romantic partner is so sure the other person should make the changes deemed important by him or her. This expectation may not have been presented to the other party or may go over like a lead balloon if it has been suggested. Psychologist and educator Andy Hogg cautions, "Don't enter a relationship planning to change the other person. You can't make someone else more affectionate, open, responsible, or sexual. You can only tell the other person what you want. People only change by their own choice. It is much more important to appreciate what you like about the person."

You may request that someone make a change, but anything beyond that is generally a violation of healthy boundaries. Relationships flourish when you accept your partner and other important people in your life for who they are instead of wanting them to change to meet your conception of what they should be. Karen Casey suggests, "Truly loving another means letting go of all expectations. It means full celebration of another's personhood." Learn to accept the other person's shortcomings. Or go one step better: appreciate their uniqueness and eccentricities. You can turn those behaviors that frustrate you into something much more acceptable. It's really your choice. Doing so not only improves relationships, it also reduces the stress in your life.

Good Will Hunting is a wonderful movie in which the title character (played by Matt Damon), is a brilliant young man whose painful past has left him scarred and afraid to get close to a special someone. He has met a young woman and he's ready to run. Sean Maguire (played by Robin Williams), is Will's psychologist, who has his own emotional challenges since the death of his wife. In one of their therapy sessions, Maguire broaches the subject of a partner's "peccadilloes."

He explains to Will: "You're not perfect sport, and let me save you the suspense, this girl you've met, she's not perfect either. But the question is whether or not you're perfect for each other. My wife used to fart when she was nervous. She had all sorts of wonderful idiosyncrasies. She used to fart in her sleep. I thought I'd share that with you. One night it was so loud it woke up the dog. She woke up and went 'ah was that you?' And I didn't have the heart to tell her. Oh! But Will, she's been dead for two years, and that's (what) I remember; wonderful stuff you know? Little things like that. Those are the things I miss the most. The little idiosyncrasies that only I know about; that's what made her my wife. Oh she had the goods on

34

me, too, she knew all my little peccadilloes. People call these imperfections, but they're not. Ah, that's the good stuff."

Don't expect people to treat you fairly according to your definition

The misguided concept that life should be fair, and all the people with whom you come in contact should treat you fairly, is nothing but trouble. The person obsessed with fairness is perpetually keeping score. Of course, what constitutes fairness in this regard is defined by each person, a perplexing problem and a trap, for sure. But I have news for you: First bulletin – the world is not fair! Second bulletin – other people may not, and probably don't, see fairness the way you do. You don't get to make the rules or control how others think.

But it will help if you understand and accept an adaptable, reasonable approach: treat others with dignity and refuse to allow anyone to mistreat you. Define mistreatment carefully and sparingly. Forget about fairness, which often involves unrealistic expectations of others and deems you the center of the universe which, of course, you are not. **Remember:** *Expectation minus reality = frustration!* Give the nutty fairness idea the heave-ho by identifying your unrealistic thoughts, expectations and beliefs about fairness and changing them to a more adaptive, reality-based understanding of your relationship to others. Honestly, it can be quite a relief to lose the "I'm the center of the universe" bit.

Don't expect the world to work the way you want it to or to treat you fairly.

People often have expectations of the world that are action stoppers. Expectations such as "the world should treat me fairly" and "the world should shower me with good luck" simply don't serve you well in your quest to reach goals and dreams. Thinking that things should happen a certain way more often than not results in disappointment. Carl Sagan, the American astronomer and author of *Cosmos: A Personal Voyage*, advises, "It is far better to grasp the Universe as it really is than to persist in delusion, however satisfying and reassuring." Do you believe that the world should treat you fairly? This unrealistic expectation prevents a lot of people from living their lives proactively. Denis Wholey speaks to this crazy notion: "Expecting the world to treat you fairly because you are a good person is a little like expecting the bull not to attack you because you are a vegetarian."

Another fanciful expectation that dampens the efforts of many individuals is the idea that the world should bless them with abounding good luck, that luck is something bestowed upon you. Yikes! Luck is a dead-end concept. Being stuck on the luck idea indicates that you believe external factors have the greatest influence on the outcomes in your life. Don Shula, the Hall of Fame coach who holds the National Football League record for the most career wins, has a more adaptive idea about what luck really is: "Sure luck means a lot in football. Not having a good quarterback is bad luck."

APPROACHES THAT ENHANCE RELATIONSHIPS

Pay attention to what others do well

As statesman and naturalist Sir John Lubock posits, "What we see depends mainly on what we look for." Let me give you an example of the importance and power of where you direct your focus. I've worked with many parents over the years who are at their wit's end because their child is misbehaving, sometimes outrageously, even dangerously so. Many times I find that parents are focusing completely on what the child is doing wrong with no attention being paid to the many things the youngster is doing right. I understand that the parents feel overwhelmed and alarmed by the misbehaviors, but what they end up doing is telling the child loudly and clearly how to get their attention, albeit negative attention.

You might be surprised to know that even negative attention can be quite reinforcing! I tell parents that they are often considered by the child to be the "best game in town," that for the child it can be fun to misbehave and then watch the parents go crazy! When I inquire about the child's positive behaviors, so many times I'm told there aren't any to report. Now, unless the child is Damien in *The Omen*, I suggest to the parents that we need to look harder. Obviously the child's good deeds, times of calm and reasonable behavior are getting no attention at all. The parents are usually quite surprised by the changes in the child's behavior when they pay less attention to the negative behavior and more to the positive. The clinical advice is "Catch them doing good." This same principal works equally well in adult relationships. Focusing on another's strengths and positive attributes opens the door for new, more adaptive expectations. This approach fosters acceptance and gratitude, both of which are key elements in flourishing relationships.

Acceptance

The Swiss psychiatrist, Carl Jung, maintains, "We cannot change anything until we accept it. Condemnation does not liberate, it oppresses." Acceptance means loving another for who they are and for the choices they are making for themselves. When you're practicing acceptance you see yourself and the other person as whole individuals who don't need anything from each other in order to be happy. When you accept another you understand that there is no need to be jealous and that the differences among people are not obstacles but rather opportunities to learn, grow and deepen the relationship. Sir Walter Besant contends, "Tolerance is the eager and glad acceptance of the way along which others seek the truth."

Arthur Gordon tells us, "Some people confuse acceptance with apathy, but there's all the difference in the world. Apathy fails to distinguish between what can and what cannot be helped; acceptance makes that distinction. Apathy paralyzes the will-to-action; acceptance frees it by relieving it of impossible burdens." Acceptance involves a change of focus. Your focus shifts from judgment to appreciation and from your needs to the health of the relationship. This reduces conflict and encourages the integrity of your interactions. It's a path to becoming a better listener, a better partner, a happier individual. "Being happy doesn't mean that everything is perfect. It means that you've decided to look beyond the imperfections" (Author Unknown).

Accepting others for themselves, warts and all, frees you from the frustrations and resentments that tie your emotions in knots. Acceptance is kind, understanding and present-focused. Acceptance is certainly contagious. When you accept all the facets of your partner, your parent, your friend or your child, you create an atmosphere of peace and harmony. More often than not, this approach evokes more positive acceptance and behavior from the other person. Martin Luther King, Jr. maintains, "The art of acceptance is the art of making someone who has just done you a small favor wish that he might have done you a greater one."

Gratitude enhances our relationships

There is one change a person can make that will almost invariably lead to more robust and deeper relationships: the practice of gratitude. The ability to experience and express gratitude can enhance relationships in amazing ways. Melodie Beattie believes, "Gratitude unlocks the fullness of life. It turns what we have into enough, and more. It turns denial into acceptance, chaos into order, confusion into clarity. It turns problems into gifts, failures into success, the unexpected into perfect timing, and mistakes into important events. Gratitude makes sense of our past, brings peace for today and creates a vision for tomorrow."

Gratitude imbues a relationship with energy and enthusiasm. When your focus is one of appreciation of what you have and the qualities of the people in your life, your thoughts, feelings and behaviors become more loving and more positive. It's far easier to practice empathy and be a good listener. Gratitude deepens the love between two people. When tough times occur, as they do for everyone, gratitude gives you a more adaptive perspective on the ups and downs, allowing you to keep the focus on the gifts of life and love. And gratitude makes it less likely that you'll take the other person for granted, or if you do, that it will be short-lived.

Albert Einstein suggests, "There are only two ways to live your life. One is as though nothing is a miracle. The other is as though everything is a miracle." Gratitude is an attitude, a focusing on the good and the defocusing from problems and resentments. It's an adjustment of expectations to match what's reasonable and possible. It promotes kindness and understanding. To adopt this attitude, take time to think about the other person's strengths, all those things the person does that make a difference. Be grateful for the things that make someone else exactly who he or she is. Enjoy and be mindful of the feelings that come from appreciation of another human being. And for goodness sakes, communicate your gratitude!

Practicing gratitude takes time and plenty of persistence. And just in case your motivation ebbs now and then, remember the metaphor from George Bernard Shaw: "A Native American elder once described his own inner struggles in this manner: 'Inside of me there are two dogs. One of the dogs is mean and evil. The other dog is good. The mean dog fights the good dog all the time.' When asked which dog wins, he reflected for a moment and replied, 'The one I feed the most.'" And such is the case with gratitude, the more you feed it, the more it brings sunshine to you and those around you.

GRATITUDE EXERCISES

The Gratitude Visit from "Eudemonia, the Good Life: A Talk with Martin Seligman," The Edge Foundation (2004)

Hundreds of people have gone through "the gratitude visit." In the gratitude visit you think of someone in your life who made an enormous positive difference, who's still alive, whom you never properly thanked. To make a gratitude visit, do the following: First, write a 300-word testimonial to a person who has been special in your life; make it concrete, telling the story of what this person did, how it made a difference, and where you are in life now as a result. Then call him up and ask to visit. If he wants to know why, just say, "It's a surprise." And when you show up at his door, sit down, and read the testimonial. Not surprisingly, it turns out that everyone weeps when this happens. Check your happiness levels before, right after the visit and three and six months later. Ask yourself, "are you happier? Are you less depressed?" The gratitude visit is one of the exercises that can diminish depression and increase happiness for a long time.

Three Blessings/Gratitude Journal Exercise
Seligman, M. (2002), Authentic Happiness; Emmons, R. (2007)
Thanks!: How the Science of Gratitude Can Make You Happier

Each night before bed, write down at least three things that went well that day. Writing about gratitude can increase appreciation and the memory of your blessings. If your list becomes repetitive, list the different components of each benefit, and reflect on each separately. Mentally label each benefit "a gift." Making this exercise a habit can increase happiness and decrease depression.

Thank Everyone for Everything Practice: Frisch, M. (2005),
Quality of Life Therapy

Establish an ongoing practice of expressing gratitude. Actively watch for things that others do that are kind, helpful, and considerate. Thank them overtly. It can help to send a card or an e-mail. The idea is not to get something back. The act of saying thanks serves others and is its own reward. Accept gratitude from others graciously. For colleagues and others seen every day, picture yourself building up a "Bank Account of Good Will."

Chapter 5
IMPRISONED BY FEAR?

"You gain strength, courage and confidence by every experience in which you really stop to look fear in the face…. You must do the thing you think you cannot do."
Eleanor Roosevelt

The FEAR BELIEF: My life is governed by fear, so I have to worry about and avoid those things that scare me.

This belief is a problem if you tell yourself:

o Most of what happens to me is beyond my control
o I believe I am not as brave and capable as others
o Feeling safe is the most important thing in the world to me
o Having security and staying in my comfort zone is far more important than taking chances that might lead to something better
o I should be scared to death to take risks that could change my life in unexpected ways.
o It would be disastrous if I made a wrong decision, made a mistake or failed at something
o I will be devastated and unable to cope if something difficult or traumatic happens to me
o The unknown is to be feared and avoided
o It is better for me to avoid conflict with others because it might hurt them, disappoint them or make them angry at me
o Because conflict with others is so uncomfortable for me, I should avoid it
o I believe it is important to stay the course in relationships, no matter how dysfunctional
o Change is something to be avoided when possible
o I believe "the devil you know is easier to take than the devil you don't know."
o It is easier to avoid many of life's problems and fears than to face them
o If something bad might happen, I should worry about it so I'm prepared

o If something bad might happen I should worry about it to make it less likely

For too many individuals, fear is paralyzing and, when allowed, can rule with an iron fist. The internal world and actions of a fearful person are governed by a phantom tyrant. Many of us capitulate to its perceived power, often without much resistance. This capitulation to fear is malignant to the human spirit, robbing one of dignity, happiness and hope. The power it wields is shear chicanery existing only because an individual acquiesces, becoming its prisoner. According to Ralph Waldo Emerson, "Fear defeats more people than any one thing in the world."

Fear is one of the emotional/physical pathways we experience when the old, **non-thinking** part of the brain perceives that a situation is life-threatening. The other pathway is aggression. The fear reaction sets the body in motion to run or escape from the threat, while the aggression reaction sets the body in motion to fight. This "fight or flight response" is essential in truly dangerous circumstances to decrease the chance of injury or death. The key word here is "perceives." The perception that a situation is life-threatening does not mean that it is. And therein lies the rub. Most of us have experienced fear in circumstances that do not threaten our safety. But our body acts like a big old bear is chasing us down a mountain! The response is the same as in the days of the cavemen. It is, however, our interpretation of the situation – what we tell ourselves about the potential consequences – instead of a real threat of danger that has become the trigger. Arnold Glasow contends, "Fear is the lengthened shadow of ignorance."

What are these fears that immobilize and debilitate us needlessly? Some people fear making mistakes, or even more catastrophic, failing in any way. Just the thought can generate a panic attack. Others will do just about anything to avoid disapproval, embarrassment or rejection. Then there is fear of the unknown, which, of course, is far reaching since there are so many unknowns in life. There's fear of success -- what an action-stopper that can be. Some people are afraid of both failure and success! Fear of change and the possible loss of control that can accompany it, even if for a

42

short time, can profoundly intimidate some people. And on and on it goes. Some folks move from one fear to another and another and another. I find it exhausting and depressing just thinking about how hard it is to live this way. Michael Pritchard warns us, "Fear is that little darkroom where negatives are developed."

In the event that you allow yourself to be governed by fear, to lack the courage to proactively live the life that's congruent with your vision, there are many negative consequences you can anticipate. The likelihood of getting what you want is markedly decreased. As Nora Roberts asserts, "If you don't go after what you want, you'll never have it. If you don't ask, the answer is always no. If you don't step forward, you'll always be in the same place." This positions you to assume the helpless role, leaving you with fewer and fewer choices. Sooner or later you will likely experience disappointment and haunting regrets about numerous lost opportunities. These regrets pile up, and before you know it, all you can think about is what you have lost and cannot regain. You keep paying dearly for your fear of fear. And sadly, this defeatist, fear-driven approach is often passed from generation to generation. Indeed, those who give in to fear are controlled from without, not from within, and their ability to garner what is resplendent in this life is severely limited.

Timothy Luce asserts, "The brave don't live forever, but the cautious don't live at all. Here's to the brave!" Indeed. Facing your fears takes courage, sometimes mounds of courage. Courage for many people represents something quite daunting, but in reality, it's not nearly as elusive and difficult as many believe. Psychological courage propels a person from powerless to robust and increases exponentially the ability to transform an impossible dream into a mission accomplished. Walt Disney, the great dream maker, believes that "all our dreams can come true if we have the courage to pursue them."

I love watching the 150 watt light bulb go on during a person's journey forward, experiencing the epiphany that facing your fears and refusing to be helpless makes you a mighty force for enacting your vision. The process of learning to take risks and act boldly is truly awesome, the gift that keeps on giving. This is a gift you give yourself and one you offer to others by your example. Fear, like hunger, is nature's way of insuring survival of the species. It's a distinct part of our human wiring, not something that should be a source of shame. What counts is your attitude and behavior when faced with the uncomfortable feelings of the fear response, which can range in intensity from mild to extreme. What matters is what you tell yourself and what you do about it.

Believing that you can face your fears and dictate how your life will be is a prerequisite to taking control. You must be willing to do what it takes to shape your life in the direction of your goals in spite of fear. As Mark Twain contends, "Courage is resistance to fear, mastery of fear, not the absence of fear." And Ambrose Moon believes, "Courage is not the absence of fear but rather the judgment that something else is more important than fear."

THE BENEFITS OF PSYCHOLOGICAL COURAGE

What do you gain by becoming psychologically courageous? You gain yourself. There is a wonderful freedom that comes from being brave and facing your fears. Unchallenged fear is a prison that progressively depletes your world of choices as you comply repeatedly with its dictates. Avoidance leads to more avoidance, forcing a long and arduous detour from a fulfilling, fruitful life. Just as avoidance leads to more avoidance, courageous thoughts and actions lead to more courageous thoughts and actions. As a psychologist, I have worked with so many people whose lives were tied up in knots by their uncontested fears and by the difficulties of not knowing how to manage stress. When you embrace the courage it takes to meet your fears with action and resolve, you get the opportunity to be the person you want to be. Anais Nin, the French author, contends, "Life shrinks or expands in proportion to one's courage." Courage fosters creativity, happiness, integrity, social connections, optimism and resilience. Remarkably, courage turns change from a fear stimulus to a "field of dreams," helping in the discovery of your power within.

How you feel about yourself and your place in this world is greatly affected by whether you take the path of surrendering to fear or the path of becoming courageous. As an unknown author wisely states, "An inferiority complex is a conviction by your fears." Courage nourishes self-confidence, self-respect and self-efficacy. Saying no to the path of avoidance, the alluring, deceptive path of least resistance, and choosing the path of forward motion can be a transformative decision for an individual. Each time you take on something you fear, even if in small increments, you learn of your strengths and potential. This translates into confidence and self-reliance.

Courage and happiness go hand in hand. In their book, *What Happy People Know*, Dan Baker and Cameron Stauth advise, "We need to be willing to charge headlong into the inferno of our most horrific fears – eyes open, intellect and spirit at the ready – even as our survival instincts are screaming, 'Run! Run! Get out!' That takes courage, and that's why courage is one of the prerequisites for happiness."

Creativity and success belong to those who face their fears. Both require the willingness to take leaps into the unknown, to continue to believe in yourself and your goals when others offer only discouragement. Both creativity and success are born of adventurousness and the understanding that it often pays off to flirt with the impossible. As President Franklin Delano Roosevelt contends, "The only limit to our realization of tomorrow will be our doubts of today."

Courage is the gift we give to others by our example. In a moving tribute to her husband, Eleanor Clift, the political commentator and contributing editor to *Newsweek* magazine, told of his courage and its effect on others in his battle with kidney cancer in an article published April 1, 2005. In this impassioned article, she tells us that her husband was a man who early in their marriage had difficulty handling sinus infections, but that somehow when facing this devastating illness he displayed the courage, spirit and clarity that was a gift to her and others. He convinced her to join him on the Diane Rehm radio broadcast to discuss his journey and answer questions in an attempt to help others facing such circumstances. At first reluctant, she decided that she had to find the courage to do this with him. The public response was heartening: "So many people have mentioned hearing us and gaining strength and courage from Tom's unflinching responses."

THE MALIGNANCY OF AVOIDANCE

When you avoid something that scares you, those fearful feelings and the accompanying physical symptoms often diminish or disappear altogether. When you avoid something that's distasteful or boring, the absence of the negative or boring situation actually reinforces the avoidant behavior.

Because the behavior of avoiding or escaping is so powerful in halting that which is distressing, distasteful or boring, it becomes more likely that you'll use this response again when the same or a similar situation presents itself. Avoidance has gained strength, and you are in backward motion. Avoidance leads to more avoidance. When this is the case, you have limited or lost your control in this area. You are caught up in a cognitive, emotional and behavioral state of confusion.

Let's say that you are fearful of public speaking. You've agreed to give a presentation, but just the thought of standing in front of a large audience gives you heart palpitations, gas, sweaty palms and thoughts of moving to Australia. You put off practicing the speech because even practicing makes you feel ill. You make a phone call to cancel or reschedule your commitment with the lame excuse of having some disease one can only contract in a remote village in Africa.

When you hang up from the call, your heart palpitations and gas disappear, your sweaty palms become dry, and your thoughts are focused on what you are going to have for lunch. Avoidance in the moment has aborted your fearful symptoms. The avoidant behavior has gained power in this situation, and in the future the likelihood of using this course of action has increased, sometimes markedly. Avoidance controls you. In terms of your public speaking fear, persistence has been dealt a blow. It's much like drinking alcohol in the morning to treat your hangover. This intervention may reduce your symptoms, but I can guarantee that you're not in control, the alcohol is in control.

So what's wrong with strategies that make you feel better, even if just in the short-term? What's wrong with managing fear and aversive situations in this way? The answer is important. Your behavior is reactive, not proactive. You're not going toward your power, you're moving away from it. You have limited your choices. This backward spiraling may take on a life of its own. It can become infectious, spreading or generalizing to other parts of your life. I have seen the far-reaching effects of avoidance many, many times. These effects can result in one's own personal incarceration. Fortunately, this pattern can be turned around. You can become proactive and regain control.

For many years, from childhood to graduate school, I too was horrified by public speaking. On a rational level, I realized that this was a very common fear, but I still believed beyond a doubt that my case was special, that for some reason I was more terrorized by this than anyone in history. Just the thought of presenting in front of a group made me feel incredibly sick. Now that I have worked for so many years with clients who are fearful, I realize many people feel like their reactions are beyond the usual human experience.

Anyway, I was forced to overcome this fear because professors are not very understanding of graduate students with this problem -- or any other problem for that matter. The real day of reckoning came when my supervising professor signed me up to give a lecture to a psychology association membership. On the way to the talk, I actually thought about being in a minor car accident and how that might be preferable to showing up! Not that I would intentionally do such a ridiculous thing, but how crazy is that? Think about it. I imagined how great it would be to have some sort of acceptable excuse to avoid my fear rather than stand and talk to people who had no reason to hurt me! When I work with clients I reflect on that day; and the very vivid memory keeps my empathy flowing.

I'm delighted to tell you that fear is very treatable and, in most cases, without a therapist. The principles and tools are pretty straightforward. Keep in mind that you're dealing with the "fight or flight response." Abundant research and clinical work have availed strategies that can empower you to take on your fear and manage it quite well. This is true even if you have an anxiety disorder that may make this response even more challenging. I learned the strategies, and they have served me well… a relief indeed!

People with anxiety disorders generally have a heightened reaction to certain fear-evoking situations. The reaction may be triggered more quickly, may last longer, or may be greater in intensity than would be the effect on the rest of us. The same strategies are used for managing these heightened reactions with a significant success rate. People with anxiety disorders often need professional help to manage the condition optimally.

MANAGING FEAR AND DEVELOPING COURAGE

Identifying your particular area or areas of fear is a very important first step. Below you will find some of the most common fear situations and challenges:

Making difficult choices and taking risks

Helen Keller believes, "Security is mostly a superstition. It does not exist in nature… Life is either a daring adventure or nothing." Making bold choices involves learning to tolerate, even enjoy, the prospect of unknown results. It's an attitude of wonder, not fear of the unpredictable. Making difficult or bold choices teaches us to look at the plethora of possibilities. And with each choice that's made, we are rewarded with strength and self-confidence, even if the choice does not work out as well as we had hoped. According to Harvey Mackay, author of *Swim with the Sharks without Being Eaten Alive*, "There are lots of ways to become a failure, but never taking a chance is the most successful."

Taking risks can alert the brain to engage its alarm system. But keep in mind that when you're not held hostage by this primitive system, you become the engineer of you existence. Start with one small risk.

Follow through, and after you've taken a deep breath, choose another to pursue.

Facing interpersonal conflict

Interpersonal conflict has a chilling, incapacitating impact on many people. Once a person starts avoiding or retreating from conflict, this pattern of avoidance and escape gets a heavy dose of reinforcement. Left unaddressed, this pattern wields a destructive influence on your ability to succeed in your goals and dreams. Bottom line, whatever you avoid due to fear stops you cold in your tracks.

A husband hates getting into arguments with his wife. She's much quicker at comebacks and can be quite the bully. As a child he hated hearing his parents argue and then came the disturbing silence for what seemed like an eternity to a small boy. The husband has learned to keep his mouth shut regarding opinions that dissent with his wife's views. In this way he avoids the discomfort of conflict and silence and spares his child from the fear and sadness he felt growing up. His avoidance is reinforced by peace at home.

Sound okay? No way. This husband has convinced himself that psychological cowardice is his best course. It's not. He is not standing up for himself. He has adopted a role of emotional impotence that almost always fosters resentment and difficulty in relationships. To add to the dysfunctional effects, the husband is setting an unhealthy example for his child, an example of acquiescing again and again. Abraham Maslow, the American psychologist believes, "Conflict itself is, of course, a sign of health as you would know if you ever met really apathetic people, really hopeless people, people who have given up hoping, striving, coping."

I stipulate that conflict is best handled with fair fighting skills and rules. The husband and his wife in my example need to learn assertiveness and conflict resolution. Ann Landers subscribes to the belief that, "All married couples should learn the art of battle as they should learn the art of making love. Good battle is objective and honest – never vicious or cruel. Good battle is healthy and constructive and brings to a marriage the principal of equal partnership."

Developing a proactive attitude toward difficulties

A person's attitude about failure and difficulties has a commanding effect on the vim and vigor of psychological courage. If you believe that failure is shameful or unfair and difficulties are something to cry over, then courage will be sadly compromised in your repository of strengths. After all, you can choose to allow life's stuff to beat you down and depress you, or you can take to heart the words of Leonardo Da Vinci: "Obstacles cannot crush me; every obstacle yields to firm resolve." It takes courage to keep moving in spite of life's "to be expected" arduous downturns and troubles.

Your attitude toward obstacles, criticism, setbacks, mistakes and failure is very important. Being afraid of encountering any of these, avoiding them whenever possible, is an entirely counterproductive approach. Victor Frankl, author of *Man's Search for Meaning*, explains, "What a man needs is not a tensionless state but rather the striving and struggling for some goal worthy of him. What he needs is not the discharge of tension at any cost, but the call of potential meaning waiting to be fulfilled by him."

I can promise you that 95% of the time you're working toward a goal, you will experience at least one, but more likely many, of the above. It's your job in becoming persistent to normalize these, that is, see them as an inevitable part of the process, not a catastrophe. They are as common as inclement weather for you, me and everyone! Who in the world told you that goal achievement is supposed to come easily, quickly and without some bruises and cuts – sometimes deep cuts? If that's the assumption you have, it's time to change your mind. Instead of feeling sorry for yourself, refuse to be discouraged by failures, delays, difficulties, mistakes and other prickly interruptions.

Courage is born of understanding and accepting that life, with its dreams and goals, is often messy, difficult and painful. But for goodness sakes, take heart in what Christopher Robin said to Pooh:

"Promise me you'll always remember you're braver than you believe, and stronger than you seem, and smarter than you think." Change your internal dialogue. You can get out of the avoidance trap by viewing difficulties as challenges replete with all sorts of possibilities. Change your self-talk. Utilize strong statements to dispute the cognitions that immobilize your plans and dreams.

Ending unhealthy relationships

Eleanor Roosevelt said, "You gain courage and confidence by every experience in which you really stop to look fear in the face. You are able to say to yourself, 'I have lived through this horror. I can take the next thing that comes along.' You must do the thing you think you cannot do."

Many people find themselves in complicated, abusive relationships where fear and uncertainty are pervasive, where the choice to end the situation is fraught with unknown, potentially negative consequences. The woman without financial options whose husband beats her and the children has to look long and hard for the backbone to leave. Her problems are overwhelming; after all, how will they survive without an income? What if he comes after them in a rage? Or the teenager who's lonely and embarrassed not to have a boyfriend; she believes something is wrong with her if she's not involved in a relationship. Her current partner is kind now and then, but most of the time he tells her she's a loser and too fat. She wonders, "Isn't any kind of boyfriend better than no boyfriend at all?"

And then there's the man whose father has criticized him since childhood; he has tried every way he knows to please and impress this man – painfully, to no avail. If his father cannot love him, he thinks maybe he is unlovable. These are the relationships that need to be modified, even terminated. They are toxic. It takes tremendous courage to do what needs to be done. Professional help is often warranted in such cases.

Facing psychological, emotional and medical problems

I have spent a great portion of my professional life treating people with psychological problems. I can tell you that facing one's psychological and emotional demons requires profound courage. Whether it's the woman with panic disorder who feels like she's having a heart attack each time she drives her children to school; or the person with bipolar disorder who's on a roller coaster ride of mania followed by deep depression; or the little boy who hears voices; or the man who was abused as a child and still suffers from the trauma, courage is mandatory for these people in their quest to improve mental health.

Committing to treatment and doing what needs to be done invariably present monumental challenges that so often evoke sheer terror. I take my hat off to anyone who finds the courage for such an important endeavor. Those of us who have not been plagued with these conditions may never really understand the magnitude of courage that one must muster to do what needs to be done.

Facing medical problems, too, often presents gargantuan challenges that require enormous courage and resolve. Undergoing painful and frightening procedures, taking medications that have untoward side effects, experiencing physical limitations, waiting for what seems like an eternity for potentially life-altering answers, or receiving a frightening prognosis exemplify only some of the experiences in which one's courage will be put to the ultimate test. Courage is facing these challenges and at the same time continuing to live each day to the fullest. Alice M. Swain reminds us, "Courage is not the flowering oak that sees storms come and go; it is the fragile blossom that opens in the snow."

Making important habit changes

Habits are not, in and of themselves, negative. Many of the habits we have serve us well. It's not possible, and definitely not convenient, to have to think about everything we do day in and day out. Brushing your teeth in the morning and after each meal is done automatically;

it has become a habit. There are some habits, however, that do not serve us well.

Some are pesky, little habits like nail biting that we would prefer to eliminate; some are bad habits that have a moderately negative effect on our health, well-being and goal achievement, such as eating more food than we need or working too much or not getting enough exercise. Then there are some habits that are highly destructive in our lives and in the lives of those close to us. It takes courage, in some cases huge quantities of courage, to do what needs to be done to change or eliminate these habits.

Most addictions would fall into the category of needing more help than simple habit change. And often just following guidelines spelled out in a book simply is insufficient. More support and/or treatment are indicated. Conquering addictions requires great courage.

Abraham Lincoln declares, "Always bear in mind that your own resolution to succeed is more important than any other one thing." Do NOT be discouraged if you have met with little or no success in building new positive habits or reforming old negative habits. To be courageous in this context often requires specific information and a persistent attitude to get the job done. I love that commercial about trying to stop smoking. A kind voice says, "All those other times you tried, maybe they were just practice."

Making change an ally instead of an adversary

You have a choice in how you view, react to and utilize change. You can be afraid, hoping that very little will be different from what you have come to expect, or you can welcome change as one of your best friends. Either way, change will come, whether you like it or not. Outside factors just don't stay the same! The inability to be flexible and adapt to change is often one of the main reasons people have trouble reaching their true potential. They hold fast to ideas and ways that are part of the past. They stubbornly cling to their right to forever live in the past. They're afraid to welcome and adjust to the new because it's often fraught with unknowns. Hazel Henderson, evolutionary economist and author of *Building a Win-Win World*, suggests, "If we recognize that change and uncertainty are basic principles, we can greet the future and the transformation we are undergoing with the understanding that we do not know enough to be pessimistic."

So the question becomes how can you make change work to improve your life? First, you need to believe what Price Pritchett surmises "Change always comes bearing gifts." That's the focus of the person who leaves fear behind and proceeds to possibilities. Think of the gifts and always expect that change is on its way. Change is our ally. Change provides phenomenal opportunities. Eric Hoffer, the author of *The Ordeal of Change,* tells us, "In times of change, learners inherit the Earth, while the learned find themselves beautifully equipped to deal with a world that no longer exists."

Become the person you want to be by pursuing goals and dreams

Courage fosters your belief in yourself and your belief in all the possibilities within your reach. What gets in the way of goals and dreams? Plenty of things: fear of failure, fear of success, fear of the critical opinions of others regarding your choices, preoccupation with today's obligations or yesterday's disappointments, addiction to comfort and security, inadequate attention to what your goals and dreams really are, or whatever the "excuse de jour" happens to be. But as the poet and playwright e.e. cummings maintains, "It takes courage to grow up and turn out to be who you really are."

Pursuing your goals and dreams involves a belief system that renders courage a necessity in the pursuit of a fulfilling existence. You must believe in the importance and accessibility of your most treasured aspirations, and you must be daring and determined in the chase. Dreams flourish when one has the right kind of internal conversation. You must become your own cheerleader, repeating, "It can be done, and I'm just the one who will prove it!"

Erma Bombeck, the beloved humorist and author of *At Wit's End*, says it so well: "There are people who put their dreams in a little box and say, 'Yes, I've got dreams, of course I've got dreams.' Then they put the box away and bring it out once in a while to look in it, and yep, they're still there. These are great dreams, but they never even get out of the box. It takes an uncommon amount of guts to put your dreams on the line, to hold them up and say, 'how good or bad am I?' That's where courage comes in."

SUGGESTIONS FOR BECOMING MORE COURAGEOUS

Spend time with positive, supportive, courageous people

Follow the lead of hardy people like Oprah Winfrey who says she surrounds herself with people who say "Why Not?" to her ideas. Find those folks who have demonstrated their courage and who enjoy watching others succeed. Learn to model courage for those you care about.

Be aware of people in your world who discourage you in your important quest. Develop ways to neutralize their dissuasions. Assertiveness skills can be helpful in preparing you to speak up to those who attempt to deter you from your path of courage. Practice disputing the objections and discouragement of others, both the ones you anticipate in your head and the ones actually hurled at you. Information on assertiveness and disputing can be found in the last chapter of this book.

Believe that you are able to do what needs to be done

Initially, it can be very difficult to believe you have what it takes to complete this mission, but I promise you do. Repeat again and again a positive statement about your ability to work this through. At first you may not believe it, but if you repeat again and again, it will take hold and you will eventually know it's true. Just remember that the negative, fearful statements that you've made to yourself over time had become habits by repetition.

Don't talk yourself out of action

Fearful individuals who have succumbed to the avoidance trap are masters at talking themselves out of action. Senator John McCain, in

Why Courage Matters, recommends the following: "If you do the things you think you cannot do, you'll feel your resistance, your hope, your dignity, and your courage grow stronger every time you prove it. You will someday face harder choices that very well might require more courage. You're getting ready for them. You're getting ready to have courage. And when those moments come, unbidden but certain, and you choose well, your courage will be recognized by those who matter most to you. When your children see you choose, without hesitating, without remark, to value virtue more than security, to love more than you fear, they will learn what courage looks like and what love it serves, and they will dread its absence."

Practice, practice, practice

You can make courage a habit by doing it again and again and again. Plan to do at least one act a day that requires courage. Ruth Gordon tells us, "Courage is very important. Like a muscle, it is strengthened by use." And Aristotle explains, "We are what we repeatedly do. Excellence, then, is not an act, but a habit."

Stop thinking of yourself as a victim

Identify instances in your thinking and imagery in which you have ordained yourself the dreaded victim. Use distraction and disputing techniques (last chapter of this book) to challenge these clearly counterproductive thoughts and images. In this world, the victim mentality is an impediment to productive self-control and certainly to the strength of courage. Develop visual imagery and a dialogue in which you are powerful, determined, brave and successful.

Learn to manage the stress response

The more control you have over your body and its emergency gear, the more likely you are to face your fears and make bold choices.

Identify cognitions that feed fear and block forward progress

Use the cognitive techniques -- distraction and disputing -- to reduce, eliminate or replace the fear cognitions. For a week, keep a record of fear and negatively based thoughts and images. Identify their frequency, duration and the circumstances under which they occur. Circumstances or triggers can include times of day, interactions with others, situations where things do not go your way, and so on.

Use systematic desensitization; remember that the journey can be divided into steps

This is an ongoing journey that unfolds in a step-by-step progression. According to Lao-Tzu, the Chinese philosopher, "The journey of a thousand miles begins with one step." This is especially true in terms of managing fear. Systematic Desensitization, also known as exposure therapy, is a highly effective method for managing fear/anxiety reactions to events, situations, persons or things. Joseph Wolpe, the South African psychiatrist, developed this procedure in the 1950's. Based on the classical conditioning model, this intervention is an effective treatment for phobias and anxiety disorders as well as those fear responses that do not meet the criteria for a clinical diagnosis. The instructions for Systematic Desensitization can be found in Chapter 9.

Chapter 6
MISSING THE MARK ON HAPPINESS?

"Most folks are about as happy as they make up their minds to be."
Abraham Lincoln

The HAPPINESS BELIEF: My happiness depends on the circumstances in my life and how other people treat me.

This belief is a problem if you tell yourself:

o Certain things have to happen in my life in order for me to be happy
o I need to have money to be happy
o Rich people are happier than people with less money
o When I find a life partner, I will be happy
o When I have a baby I'll be happy
o When I have a big house or new car, etc. I'll be happy
o When I become famous I'll be happy
o When something good happens in my life it will make me really happy for a long time
o Happiness is something to search for
o You're either a happy person or you're not
o Really happy people are happy most of the time

Many of us have beliefs about happiness that just don't square with reality. Some of the research findings on happiness may well seem counterintuitive. That's the thing about research, sometimes it discovers expected relationships and sometimes it discovers relationships that are hard for us to fit into our philosophy about how things work.

Keep in mind that just because you believe something doesn't make it so. Just because you think you know how things work doesn't mean that you do. The research on happiness has given us many substantial clues on how we can increase our levels. With an open mind, a yen for discovery and the right information, you can be a happier person.

Why is happiness so important? Besides the positive emotions that are highly reinforcing in themselves, happiness brings many other gifts. Happy people are more creative, more productive, healthier physically and psychologically, earn more money, have more friends, and are more successful at staying married than folks who aren't so happy. In effect, happiness is not simply an end but a potent means as well (1). People who reported being happier are more socially involved, more likable, have higher self-esteem, have greater resilience when faced with adversity, and are less affected by negative advertising and biased thinking. They are better leaders and negotiators. Happy people aren't hung up on the successes of others. They don't compare themselves to others, whereas unhappy people make a lot of social comparisons. Happy people have a reserve of psychological energy that helps them accomplish their goals (2). And as if that's not enough, happy people have better immune function and live longer (3)!

WHAT FACTORS ARE IMPORTANT IN ACHIEVING HAPPINESS?

It turns out that happiness, like so many things in this life, is greatly affected by both nature and nurture. Sonja Lyubomirsky in *The How of Happiness* (2007), represents the three major influences on happiness as parts of a pie. She points out that biology accounts for approximately 50 percent of the pie, that each of us has a set point of inherited ability to be happy that lies somewhere between zero and 50 percent. This potential for happiness is a baseline that one returns to after difficulties and victories. Some people have a high level, some a low level and some in-between.

For those who have a high level it appears they have an easier time achieving happiness because of the point at which they start. Another part of the pie, a mere 10 percent, is the result of our circumstances. That's right -- only 10 percent of our happiness has anything to do with outside events, possessions, etc. The final part of the pie, the remaining 40 percent, is the part we have the opportunity to control (3). This is where our power lies and where it's important to consult the research to increase our well-being. This final part involves how we think, what we do -- how we approach each day with its opportunities and its challenges. So take heart knowing that even if you're on the lower level of the biological happiness quotient, 40 percent offers each of us all sorts of possibilities!

THE MYTH OF CIRCUMSTANCES IN THE QUEST FOR HAPPINESS

Circumstances have very little to do with our happiness levels. This comes as a major shock to many people. In my Positive Psychology classes, students respond to this information with disbelief, even deep dismay. In some cases, the response reminds me of my feelings when I learned there was no Santa Claus. This is a good example of cognitive dissonance. The information is unsettling. It's understandable that some people find this disturbing when they've attached their hopes to the specific circumstances they believe will bring joy to their lives.

The person who believes that circumstances bring happiness or despair thinks something like this: I'll be happy when I become a teenager, or when I turn 21, or when I get my college degree or a good paying job, or when I get married, or own a house, or when I'm rich or the kids are grown up or when I retire. I think you get the picture. In these situations, the person is waiting and anticipating that when something happens or comes her way, greater joy will result and will be ongoing. Waiting to be happy is a misguided way to find your bliss. There's a great line from *The Music Man*: "Pile up too many tomorrows and you'll find that you collected nothing but a bunch of empty yesterdays." And Henry David Thoreau warns, "As if you could kill time without injuring eternity."

Why do life's changes account for so little? "Hedonic adaptation" is the reason that circumstances matter so marginally in our levels of happiness. Hedonic is from the Greek word "h donikos," which means pleasure. We adapt to pleasurable events, and they become neutral in terms of happiness. Their effects aren't as great and don't last as long as we expected. So if you believe that losing all that weight or getting married to your soul mate is going to make you deeply happy for a long time, the research indicates that your beliefs are unrealistic.

60

The happiness effects of marriage, for example, subside after two years according to a large study in Germany that followed 25,000 people for 15 years (4). One exception is having children and watching them grow (3). We also adapt to negative events, so our predictions about the effects of misfortune on our happiness are overblown. People project that becoming crippled or having a life-threatening disease will affect them negatively in profound ways, when actually most people adapt better and more quickly than anticipated (9).

Having money, even being very wealthy, contributes only minimally to happiness levels. I've found that many folks find this very difficult to believe. Once a person's basic needs are met, additional income adds little to happiness. That's right, people with material wealth aren't as happy as you might think. In fact, the richest Americans who earn $10 million or more annually are only marginally happier than office or blue collar workers.

Money often brings problems to the rich. In a large study of wealthy adults, more than half reported that wealth didn't bring more happiness and a third of those with assets greater than $10 million said that money brought more problems than it solved. The research distinguishes between life satisfaction and happiness. Life satisfaction, that is, the way you assess your life in general, is highly connected to wealth. However, wealth has very little to do with positive emotions and personal enjoyment (3,5).

Many of us believe that being young, living in a warm, sunny place, being physically attractive, being intelligent and well-educated or being healthy bring us greater happiness. None of these factors appreciably increases happiness levels. So if these aren't the ways to happiness, how do we increase our chances?

WHAT YOU CAN DO TO BE HAPPIER

In comparison to those who are unhappy, happy people have some distinct things they do that make a difference. According to Lyubomirsky, we can increase our happiness levels by our intentional activities -- those things we do and the ways we think day in and day out. In her book, *The How of Happiness*, the "Person-Activity Fit Diagnostic Inventory" asks questions about intentional activities that an individual would enjoy doing and that would feel most natural. The questionnaire identifies the four activities that have the greatest probability of helping the particular individual augment her well-being (3). The 12 happiness intentional activities are:

Practice gratitude

Gratitude is an amazing strength that increases happiness and reduces depression. Frederick Koenig suggests, "We tend to forget that happiness doesn't come as a result of getting something we don't have, but rather of recognizing and appreciating what we do have." Counting your blessings and expressing gratitude for the benevolence of others and for the gifts we have has large effects on mood and feelings of happiness.

In a study by Seligman and colleagues at the University of Pennsylvania, 50 severely depressed individuals were instructed to log on to a website and write down three things for which the participant felt grateful each day, such as: the sun came out today; I read a chapter in a book my therapist suggested; or, I had phone call from a friend. Within 15 days, 94% of the subjects reported feeling considerably less depressed as measured on a depression inventory. These results are comparable to those achieved by medication and psychotherapy. When checked at six months, the results were maintained (6,7). Imagine that -- a simple self-administered intervention that reaped such impressive results!

The practice of gratitude can increase happiness levels by around 25 percent. A few hours writing a gratitude journal over three weeks can create an effect that lasts six months or more. When blessings are counted we savor our positive life experiences, giving us greater pleasure. This also strengthens the encoding of this information in the brain. This is one particularly powerful way to counteract the marginalizing effects of hedonic adaptation (8). Below are some gratitude exercises that can make you happier and more resilient:

The Gratitude Visit from "Eudemonia, the Good Life: A Talk with Martin Seligman" The Edge Foundation (2004)

Think of someone whose kindness and presence in your life has made a real difference for you, but who has never heard you express your gratitude. Write and rewrite a Gratitude Letter (300 words) describing in concrete terms what this person did for you and how it affected your life. Visit the individual in person, if possible, and read it to him or her out loud. According to Seligman, this is one of the gratitude exercises which makes people less depressed and happier than placebo.

Three Blessings/Gratitude Journal Exercise: Seligman, M. (2002) Authentic Happiness; Emmons, R. (2007) Thanks! How the Science of Gratitude Can Make You Happier.

Each night before bed, write down at least three things that went well that day. Writing about gratitude can increase appreciation and the memory of your blessings. If your list becomes repetitive, list the different components of each benefit, and reflect on each separately. Mentally label each benefit "a gift." Making this exercise a habit can increase happiness and decrease depression.

Thank Everyone for Everything Practice: Michael Frisch, Quality of Life Therapy, 2005

Establish an ongoing practice of expressing gratitude. Actively watch for things that others do that are helpful, kind and considerate. Thank them overtly. It can help to send a card or an e-mail. The idea is not to get something back. The act of saying thanks is service to others and is its own reward. Accept thanks from others gracefully. For colleagues and others seen every day, picture yourself building up a "Bank Account of Good Will."

Live in the present and savor your positive experiences

Happiness is made possible by being in the moment. Living in the present is a choice. You get to choose where your attention is directed -- the past, the present, or the future -- and you get to decide exactly what you tune into on those channels. When you're in the moment, savoring becomes an integral part of your experience, which promotes positive emotions for longer periods. Having an open, interactive relationship with the world on a moment to moment basis offers voluminous information and greater opportunities for happiness.

Harvard psychologists collected information on the daily activities, thoughts and feelings of 2,250 volunteers to find out how often they were focused on what they were doing and what made them happiest. Their conclusion: "A human mind is a wandering mind and a wandering mind is an unhappy mind. The ability to think about what is not happening is a cognitive achievement that comes at an emotional cost... Mind-wandering is an excellent predictor of people's happiness. In fact, how often our minds leave the present and where they tend to go is a better predictor of our happiness than the activities in which we are engaged (10)."

Spend lots of time with others and develop deep and meaningful relationships

One of the biggest factors in bringing about happiness appears to be strong, personal relationships. Unhappiness can be quelled by having someone in your life who cares about you. The efforts a person puts into healing, cultivating and enjoying relationships with family and friends reap bountiful benefits in terms of positive feelings and well-being. The research suggests that it is difficult to be happy without social relationships. As Marcel Proust maintains, "Let us be grateful to people who make us happy; they are the charming gardeners who make our souls blossom."

Be kind and compassionate

A worthy goal in the quest for happiness involves practicing kindness, compassion and understanding. The Dalai Lama tells us, "If you want others to be happy, practice compassion. If you want to be happy, practice compassion." The strength of kindness has received much attention in Positive Psychology and rightly so.

Kindness makes people happier, helps them appreciate what they have, and brings them closer to others. Treating others with kindness is not a difficult endeavor and the benefits are amazing.

Kindness and compassion create an amazing feeling of being safe. Feeling safe with another human being provides the basis on which to develop deeper and more meaningful relationships, which as previously stated is one of the most effective ways to live a happy life. George Eliot emphasizes the wonder of safety in relationships: "Oh, the comfort, the inexpressible comfort of feeling safe with a person, having neither to weigh thoughts nor measure words, but pouring them all out, just as they are, chaff and grain together, certain that a faithful hand will take and sift them, keep what is worth keeping, and with a breath of kindness blow the rest away."

And what about self-kindness? When thinking of kindness many folks forget about extending this generous attitude toward themselves. For whatever reasons, their beliefs, self-talk and actions suggest disappointment and self-loathing. Interestingly enough, most of these folks treat others more kindly. And frankly, many would not allow others to talk to them the way they talk to themselves. They often have outrageous expectations and may be perfectionists, believing that mistakes and failures are shameful. This sets them up for a cycle of self-denigration and feelings of failure -- certainly no recipe for happiness. I have witnessed many times how hard people can be on themselves. My advice is to learn to treat yourself with understanding, kindness and dignity. You'll appreciate the changes that come with this attitude.

Be optimistic

Pope John XXIII advises, "Consult not your fears but your hopes and dreams. Think not about your frustrations, but about your unfulfilled potential. Concern yourself not with what you have tried and failed in, but with what is still possible for you to do." In other words, become an optimist in the most effective sense. Optimists definitely have a leg up on happiness.

Each of us has an internal, ongoing conversation; we talk to ourselves. We tell ourselves why things happen, who is to blame for the darkness, who is to credit for the light, what the past means, and what might happen in the future. The contents of your internal dialogue go a long way in determining whether your approach is optimistic or pessimistic, whether it will serve you well or hold you back, whether it will bring you possibilities or disappointment, and whether it will fortify your happiness or deplete it.

The differences between an optimist and a pessimist in these internal dialogues are quite stark. Optimists believe in their own power to make their lives and futures better, while pessimists believe that their decisions and behaviors probably won't impact future outcomes -- a condition known in psychology as "learned helplessness." Optimism is about positive, can-do beliefs, expectations, choices and strategies, about knowing you are responsible for your life. It's about learning all you can from adversity and then propelling yourself forward toward your goals and vision. It's about believing that you're not only able to survive negative circumstances, but that you can often turn them into opportunities. It's about taking credit for the things you accomplish, savoring these victories, and utilizing them as fuel for the ongoing journey toward dreams and discovery.

Christopher Peterson, the Positive Psychologist, contends that, "Optimism galvanizes people. It sets you in motion. To be optimistic in the true sense is not to wear a smile button but to be a problem-solver."

Control negative thoughts and feelings

While negative thoughts and feelings are a way of life for some people, others are besieged by them only now and then. Either way, you'll be well served in terms of your happiness levels if you get a handle on them. Negative thoughts and feelings are not a given; that is, you have a choice about what kind of thinking goes on between your ears and, consequently, what kinds of feelings you experience. Thoughts and feeling are interactive. Thinking a negative thought can lead to negative feelings, and having unchecked negative feelings can lead to negative thoughts. Fortunately, you get to decide how much time and energy you devote to these negative aspects of your life. Learning to use this power of choice takes knowledge and practice of effective approaches. If you'd like to put some time and effort into this very worthy endeavor, you can learn more about thought stopping and disputing in the last chapter of this book.

Use your strengths and abilities to weather life's storms, and believe that good things can arise from difficulty

What are your strengths, and how can they best serve you in good times or bad? How can you employ your strengths to lead a happier and more resilient life? These are the questions that Positive Psychology has been addressing for over 12 years. Individuals can find out about their strengths by filling out the Values in Action (VIA) Questionnaire on the Authentic Happiness website (http://www.authentichappiness.sas.upenn.edu/Default.aspx). The VIA Signature Strengths Survey is a 240 question survey that has been translated into Spanish and Chinese, and more than one million people have taken it. This survey measures 24 character strengths. When you take the full test, the results will indicate your five greatest character strengths.

In his book *Authentic Happiness* (2002), Martin Seligman tells us: "I believe that each person possesses several signature strengths. These are strengths of character that a person self-consciously owns, celebrates, and (if he or she can arrange life successfully) exercises every day in work, love, play and parenting.

Have dreams and goals your whole life

Having goals and dreams and striving to bring them to fruition increases happiness and brings sunshine into our lives. Stephen Covey explains, "How different our lives are when we really know what is deeply important to us, and keeping that picture in mind, we manage ourselves each day to be and do what really matters most." By setting goals, we create a feeling of hope, optimism and a desire to become active on our own behalf. Lyubomirsky tells us: "People who strive for something personally significant, whether it's learning a new craft, changing careers, or raising moral children, are far happier than those who don't have strong dreams or aspirations. Find a happy person and you will find a project (3)."

Carl Sandburg explains, "Nothing happens unless first a dream." Unleashing your imagination and its associated feelings helps you define the dream and believe the future belongs to you. When you want to pursue a goal or build a dream, do you start with an unfettered vision, or do you think of all the problems, sacrifices and effort that it's going to take to get where you want to go? The latter reminds me of a terrific response Ann Landers wrote to a man who was considering becoming a lawyer. In his letter, he lamented the fact that he was 36 years old and that he would be 40 by the time he completed law school. Ann Landers asked him how old he would be in four years if he didn't go to law school!

By an unfettered vision, I mean taking time to relax, close your eyes and imagine all the wonderful gifts you will be choosing to pursue. Don't allow any upsetting thoughts that make you fearful and unsure of yourself to invade your world; just tell yourself that you will work out the details at another time. Consider all the possibilities. Let loose that part of your brain that loves to dream.

To dream properly you have to put aside all those pesky worries. Say, for example, that you want to embark on a new career that has great potential to bring you tremendous joy and satisfaction. You start thinking about being a sports writer, how wonderful it would be to cover football, baseball, golf, etc. The idea that someone would pay you to be in such an exciting environment sounds, well, too good to be true.

Just as you're dreaming away, you get this overwhelming feeling of dread. You say to yourself, "I have to be crazy to think like this. I'll have to go back to school, be on a reduced income until I can land a position; people will think I've lost my marbles to give up my engineering job with its healthy income and stock options. I've taken myself so far in this field. People respect the work I do. What in the world am I thinking?" By ruminating about all the reasons why not, and all the obstacles and sacrifices, by caring too much what other people think, you have single-handedly changed a dream into a nightmare. Great job!

Try this instead. Set aside some time to relax. Turn off the phone. Find a spot where no one will disturb you. Get really comfortable. Close your eyes and picture yourself as that sports journalist, or whatever passionate pursuit gets you into an enjoyable, exciting dream zone. If worrisome, defeating thoughts enter your head, passively let them go by telling yourself that you'll think about these later. For now you are going to focus on the dream. Sample all the terrific possibilities that this dream has to offer. Spend 10 or 15 minutes in your reverie. Repeat this exercise often. You'll be surprised by what you learn when you allow the dream to unfold.

Manage stress

According to Hans Selye, the scientist who first identified the stress response, "It's not stress that kills us, it is our reaction to it." Managing stress makes us more resilient in tough times and in good times. It goes a long way in augmenting our happiness levels. The stress response, also known as the "fight or flight response," has been a major part of our make-up since the cave man days. It serves the vital role of compelling us to fight fiercely or flee quickly when a dangerous situation puts us in jeopardy.

When a person perceives that a circumstance is perilous, that message is swiftly conveyed to the hypothalamus, a non-thinking part of the brain that activates the sympathetic nervous system (SNS). Many changes occur in the body when the SNS is engaged. Blood pressure and heart rate increase, breathing moves from the diaphragm to the chest and blood flow shifts to the large muscles and to the brain, away from the stomach and the extremities, restricting digestion and causing the hands and feet to become cold. Muscles tighten in readiness to run or fight. Pupils dilate, the mouth becomes dry and erections become inhibited. The immune system and tissue repair are restricted.

This is nature's way of improving the survival of the species. By redirecting and heightening the body's activity, blood flow and energy, the person in crisis has the resources to run fast or fight hard, increasing the likelihood of staying alive. The changes that occur put the body into a very uncomfortable and demanding state. Should this huge drain become chronic, serious physiological and psychological problems often result.

Just as nature equipped us with a nervous system to survive calamity, it also equipped us with a nervous system to maintain a state of calm: the parasympathetic nervous system (PNS). The characteristics or actions of the PNS are largely the opposite of the SNS and, for all intents and purposes, when one is engaged, the other is disengaged. Thus, the goal of stress management is to harness the methods that promote a state of calm and that inhibit the stress response. The following strategies have been widely researched and shown to be effective:

Managing the external world

o Assertiveness
o Reducing, eliminating or learning to react differently to stressors
o Improving communication
o Eliminating self–defeating behaviors
o Having clear goals
o Managing time in positive ways

Managing your internal psychological world

Keep in mind that the message sent to the hypothalamus may be one about an actual threat or about a perceived, benign threat. You are served well by the stress response when you're actually in danger. You are not served well if your body perceives something as life-threatening when it isn't.

o Distraction
o Disputing
o Identifying beliefs as rational or irrational beliefs
o Developing appropriate expectations of yourself, others and the world

There are calming techniques that tell the brain you are not in trouble. These can be used to disengage the response or on an ongoing basis to prevent it from being elicited.

o Diaphragmatic breathing
o Guided Imagery Relaxation
o Meditation: The Relaxation Response or Insight Meditation
o Progressive Muscle Relaxation
o Biofeedback
o Hypnosis
o Yoga
o Exercise
o Smiling

Find flow

In his book, *Flow: The Psychology of Optimal Experience* (1990), Mihaly Csikszentmihalyi has identified and researched a state he calls FLOW, which commonly occurs in people when they experience a certain type of "internal order." This internal order develops when one is engrossed in a challenging activity and believes that he or she has the ability to work through it effectively. The primary goal is to master and enjoy the activity simultaneously. There is total focus and engagement in the endeavor; time slows down, and the person achieves a complete clarity of goals.

The feelings experienced are so positive that the person wants to do the activity again and again. Flow is about the way people feel when what they are doing is working so well, or they are enjoying themselves so much, that they lose themselves in the activity. Csikszentmihalyi posits three requirements for a state of flow to occur: 1) there must be clear-cut goal(s), 2) there must be fast, accurate feedback on the progress toward the goal(s), and 3) the level of challenge must be commensurate with the person's skill level. Flow can occur in many activities such as athletics, work and creative endeavors. It's about being "in the moment," being engaged, ebullient and productive.

Practice forgiveness

Malachy McCourt wisely tells us, "Resentment is like drinking poison and waiting for the other person to die." Forgiveness, conversely, is the gift you give yourself. It's one of the 24 character strengths identified by Peterson and Seligman (12). By letting go of your anger and resentment, you let go of negative emotions, allowing your energy and focus to be on more positive emotions. Forgiveness fosters happiness, physical and mental well-being and better interpersonal relationships. Forgiveness and gratitude are two sides of a coin. Just as self kindness is a positive force, so too is self-forgiveness. We all make blunders. Holding on to them prevents more positive functioning. Forgiveness is about the past, about letting go of past real or perceived transgressions that you've experienced.

Seligman suggests the following exercise as a means to broaden one's perspective on anger or resentment toward another. This exercise is also useful for forgiving yourself:

Letting Go of Grudges exercise: Choose someone against whom you have a grudge. On a blank piece of paper, draw a circle in the center and write a few words capturing the essence of the grudge. Fill the rest of the page with at least 15 blank circles. Fill each circle with a word or phrase describing something about the person for which you are grateful. Hold the page at arm's length and reflect on how the grudge gets lost in a sea of gratitude (11).

Be realistic about what to expect

It's very important for individuals to be realistic in establishing their happiness goals and expectations. Remember that "expectation minus reality equals frustration." It's unrealistic to think that happiness is everlasting bliss. Be tuned into the fact that these feelings tend to wax and wane, and expect them to be mild to moderate. This will help you stay hopeful and committed to the intentional activities that increase the probability of being happy (1).

A Positive Psychology Happiness Vignette: Happiness as an inside job (author unknown)

"A 92-year-old, petite, well-poised and proud man, who is fully dressed each morning by eight o'clock, with his hair fashionably combed and face shaved perfectly, even though he is legally blind, moved into a nursing home today. His wife of 70 years recently passed away, making the move necessary. After many hours of waiting patiently in the lobby of the nursing home, he smiled sweetly when I told him the room was ready.

As he maneuvered his walker to the elevator, I provided a visual description of his tiny room, including the eyelet sheets that had been hung on his window. 'I love it,' he stated with the enthusiasm of an 8-year-old having just been presented with a new puppy. 'Mr. Jones, you haven't seen the room; just wait,' I said. 'That doesn't have anything to do with it,' he replied. 'Happiness is something you decide on ahead of time.

'Whether I like my room or not doesn't depend on how the furniture is arranged ... it's how I arrange my mind. I already decided to love it. It's a decision I make every morning when I wake up. I have a choice; I can spend the day in bed recounting the difficulty I have with the parts of my body that no longer work, or get out of bed and be thankful for the ones that do.'"

Footnotes

1. Biswas-Diener, R. and Dean, B. (2007). *Positive Psychology Coaching: Putting the Science of Happiness to Work for Your Clients*. New Jersey: Wiley

2. Lyubomirsky, S., King, L. and Diener, E. (2005). The benefits of frequent positive affect: Does happiness lead to success? Psychological Bulletin 131: 803-855

3. Lyubomirsky, S. (2007). *The How of Happiness.* New York: Penguin Group

4. Lucas, R.E., Clark, A. E., Georgillis, Y. and Diener, E. (2003) Reexamining adaptation and the set point model of happiness. Reactions to changes in marital status. Journal of Personality and Social Psychology, 84: 527-537

5. Diener, E. and Biswas-Diener, R. (2008). *Happiness: Unlocking the Mysteries of Psychological Wealth.* Wiley-Blackwell

6. Seligman, M.E.P., Steen, T. and Peterson, C. (2005). Positive Psychology progress: empirical validation of interventions. American Psychologist, 60, 410-421.

7. Seligman, M.E.P., Rashid, T. and Parks, A. (2006). Positive Psychology therapy. American Psychologist, November, 773-788.

8. Emmons, R. (2007). *Thanks! How the New Science of Gratitude Can Make You Happier.* New York: Houghton-Mifflin Co.

9. Lyubomirsky, S. (in press). Hedonic adaptation to positive and negative experiences. In S. Folkman (Ed.), Oxford handbook of stress, health, and coping. New York: Oxford University Press.

10. Bradt, S. Wandering mind is not a happy mind. Harvard Science Nov 2010

11. Seligman, M.E.P. (2002). *Authentic Happiness.* New York: Free Press pp. 161-162

12. Peterson, C. and Seligman, M.E.P. (2004). *Character Strengths and Virtues New York*: The New Press

Chapter 7
OBSESSED WITH PERFECTION?

"Remember that fear always lurks behind perfectionism.
Confronting your fears and allowing yourself the right to be human,
paradoxically makes you a far happier and more productive person."
David Burns, psychiatrist and author of *Feeling Good, the New
Mood Therapy*

The PERFECTION BELIEF: It is vital for me and those I care
about to be perfect

This belief is a problem if you tell yourself:

o Mistakes, failures are shameful and therefore unacceptable
o I need to be perfect and successful in everything I do
o I need to be better than others in my performance
o I should avoid goals at which I might not be perfect
o If I try something and make a mistake or suffer a setback I should
quit to avoid further embarrassment
o If I can control myself and my world, the likelihood increases that
I will be perfect
o I need to be perfect in order to gain the respect and approval of
others
o Success comes more easily for others than for me
o Whatever I do is never good enough
o Anything worth doing is worth doing perfectly
o My self-worth is directly related to my performance
o Others should live up to my expectations
o I believe that those around me -- spouse, children, coworkers --
should be behave the way I think is best
o I should not show weakness
o I can't let others know how afraid I am of appearing imperfect
o If I'm not perfect I am a loser
o There is only one way to do things
o Winning is everything
o I'm not capable of living up to my standards or the standards of
others

o Others will respect me and look up to me if I do everything to perfection
o I must always be right and do the right thing

Many people believe that being perfect according to their definition is the way to live their lives in order to be highly successful, very respected, even wildly happy. Unfortunately for them, this particular set of beliefs engenders a way of life that's more likely to foster depression, difficult relationships, and fewer and more limited accomplishments. Perfectionism is an unhealthy way to live. I've witnessed the emotional turmoil of too many people who've acquired this particular belief system with its self-defeating expectations. Believing that only one outcome (the perfect one!) is acceptable is incompatible with emotional health and well-being. I've worked with many perfectionists over the years and have found that convincing them of the insidiousness of this particular mindset presents quite a challenge.

If you're a perfectionist, changing your beliefs, expectations and behaviors won't be easy, but it will open the path to greater health, happiness and self-confidence. Perfectionists generally fit into three categories: those who expect perfection from themselves, those who expect perfection from others only, and those who expect it from both themselves and others. You and the people in your world will never be perfect or attain perfection in any desired goal. It's not going to happen, no matter what. As Salvador Dali thunders, "Have no fear of perfection – you'll never reach it."

Some perfectionists are focused on what others think about them, while others are self-oriented, that is, they're focused on their own self-evaluations. And of course, some perfectionists beleaguer themselves by being obsessed by both their own approval and the approval of others. The source of such strivings is generally a sense of inadequacy and an overwhelming fear of what will happen if the perfectionist or those associated with him or her don't perform to the ultimate degree.

Expecting the impossible is a straight shot to trouble, disappointment and rocky interpersonal relationships. It consumes so much energy to follow this particular brand of dead-end thinking. Author and psychologist Harriet Braikert warns, "Striving for excellence motivates you, striving for perfection is demoralizing." Think about it for a moment. If something has to be done to a tee, there's not much room for exploration, discovery, spontaneity and joy. Costly, debilitating and not much fun! Keep in mind that the perfectionist is worried about all the details of the outcome. That's a powerful way to put out the fire and marginalize whatever gains you or anyone else can make. This also makes it hard to be open to unexpected or disguised opportunities. It affects other people adversely because it's "your way or the highway."

WHAT IS PERFECTIONISM?

A set of irrational beliefs/thinking

At its core, perfectionism is a set of beliefs that propels into motion those behaviors, expectations and perceptions that are extreme, irrational, enslaving and self-defeating. Beliefs such as "mistakes are a sign of weakness" and "failure is a catastrophe," have little to do with reality. Reality dictates that all of us make mistakes and experience failure at times. Not only that, but both mistakes and failures provide all kinds of possibilities for learning about life. Ralph Waldo Emerson reminds us, "Men succeed when they realize that their failures are the preparation for their victories."

The perfectionist's cognitive domain is often characterized by the extreme "all or nothing" thinking and the dreaded "shoulds." All or nothing thinking -- you're either a winner or a loser, you're successful or you're not, etc. -- set up a narrow band for approving of yourself or others. This is demoralizing and a drain on your energy and happiness. You develop an endless list of "shoulds" that dominate your thinking and the consequent things you do. You become a prisoner of your own thoughts and beliefs.

Inappropriate definitions

Julia Cameron tells us, "Perfectionism is not a quest for the best. It is a pursuit of the worst in ourselves, the part that tells us that nothing we do will ever be good enough - that we should try again." The perfectionist's definition of failure is unconfined, so wide and encompassing, while her definition of success is very restrictive. Think about how debilitating those definitions can be. Failing is easily achieved because so many possibilities are included in that category. Success is illusive because so few outcomes are considered acceptable. Talk about setting yourself up for defeat and feelings of helplessness!

The perfectionist thinks in absolutes. She doesn't differentiate between perfection and excellence nor take into account how learning is achieved. She's unable to see negative occurrences as opportunities for growth. Failing, overcoming obstacles, bouncing back from mistakes, handling tough times present chances to adapt to what life sends our way and discover the path toward effectiveness and stability.

Unrealistic expectations

Stanley J. Randall believes, "The closest to perfection a person ever comes is when he fills out a job application form." The perfectionist is plagued with unrealistic expectations of herself and others. She expects to be successful in every endeavor, outshine others in designated areas such as performance, appearance, accomplishments, material possessions, etc. This makes others her competition, even when competition is inappropriate. This competition can have a chilling effect on interpersonal relationships.

Relationships are also compromised by the specific expectations imposed on those around her: spouses, children, coworkers and friends -- anyone who enters the perfectionist's world may be subject to the perfectionist's credo.

Unaddressed fears

The perfectionist is afraid of so many possibilities. In fact, feared outcomes are one of the main motivations compelling the perfectionist to remain in this destructive trap. The perfectionist may fear failure, disapproval, mistakes, criticism, embarrassment, mediocrity, even success. Success can be anxiety-producing because it sets a standard that the perfectionist must then continue to meet or exceed. As an unknown author asserts, "The most difficult part of attaining perfection is finding something to do for an encore." As most of us are aware, capitulating to fear is a slippery slope. The more a person gives in to its dictates, the more powerful and pervasive it becomes. It can lead to chronic procrastination because there is a fear of completing tasks -- heaven forbid that they might be inferior -- and with their completion that will become obvious.

Compulsive needs

A compulsion is a hard-to-control impulse to do something in order to avoid those unacceptable thoughts and consequences that produce anxiety. Perfectionists are very afraid and unwilling to show their vulnerabilities. They have a strong need to be in control, which is accomplished by achievement, mastery of their expectations, domination over others and avoidance of goals that they're not very confident of completing in desired ways. This is how they manage their anxiety. Of course, all of this is done at a great cost to them and those they care about.

Anne Lamott, author of *Bird by Bird: Some Instructions on Writing and Life,* maintains: "I think perfectionism is based on the obsessive belief that if you run carefully enough, hitting each stepping-stone just right, you won't have to die. The truth is that you will die anyway and that a lot of people who aren't even looking at their feet are going to do a whole lot better than you and have a lot more fun while they're doing it."

Inappropriate/obsessive focus

"Focus of attention" is a psychological term that refers to the mind's capacity to direct its inner awareness to a specific target. Where you focus your attention makes all the difference in terms of your health and well-being. The research on mindfulness -- focusing on the here and now -- is quite compelling in terms of just how important this focus can be.

Each of us has a choice about where we focus our attention and energies. We can focus on those things that deplete our energy or on those that augment it. The perfectionist, not surprisingly, has an obsessive focus of attention on such things as the faults, the mistakes, missteps, failures of self and others and a faulty goal system that targets the unachievable. Instead of finding what is truly meaningful and important to her, the perfectionist is focused on the quest for faultlessness and ideal accomplishments and is mindless about the moment at hand. This focus produces inordinate amounts of worry and guilt -- which certainly is energy depleting.

Mindfulness, on the other hand, is about being in the present moment and viewing it non-judgmentally -- all but impossible within the perfectionist's world. In the movie *Star Trek: Generations*, Captain Jean-Luc Picard maintains, "Time is a companion that goes with us on a journey. It reminds us to cherish each moment because it will never come again. What we leave behind is not as important as how we have lived."

THE EFFECTS OF PERFECTIONISM

I read a really sad story about a perfectionist that I think embodies the lethality of this misguided thinking. The Associated Press ran an article by Melissa Nelson on January 11, 2005, entitled, "Top Surgeon kills self. Doctor treated young patients." A surgeon who was profoundly skilled in correcting heart defects in infants and children took his own life with an overdose of drugs and alcohol. According to his colleagues, he was inordinately self-critical and would obsess about the very few children he was unable to save, instead of focusing on the many he did save. He was only 45 years old; what a talent the world lost! Perfectionism can be downright perilous.

Perfectionism is a serious problem; no form of it is without a downside. Some of the problems of the perfectionist experiences are as follows:

80

Vulnerabilities

Ursula LeGuin contends, "Almost anything carried to its logical extreme becomes depressing, if not carcinogenic." Perfectionists have serious vulnerabilities to Depressive Disorders, Anxiety Disorders (especially Obsessive-Compulsive Disorder), Eating Disorders, stress-related complications and suicide. Why is this? Well, for example, perfectionists are prone to depression because of the feelings of helplessness they experience when expectations are unmet. Perfectionists strive for control but it is so often beyond their purview.

Eating Disorders are also common because of the need to be in control of body size and appearance. Anorexics are continually comparing themselves to others physically. This obsession makes it difficult to be happy with a body that doesn't match society's ideal. I remember a client of mine actually explaining that when she goes in a room full of people she finds the smallest person, and if that person is smaller than she, she becomes very upset!

Perfectionists may experience headaches, gastrointestinal difficulties, muscle tension and cardiovascular problems. They are often plagued by a pessimistic attitude, especially when their expectations and perceived abilities are at odds.

Procrastination/diminished productivity

By focusing on unrealistic goals, the perfectionist is set up for failure and diminished productivity. She may experience an overwhelming fear of failure that immobilizes her, ensnaring her in the procrastination trap. The perfectionist often feels inadequate and may not want to have this inadequacy confirmed for all to see, so she procrastinates. She may be fearful of an unsure outcome or may fear taking on an endeavor that could manifest in a flawed result. Heaven forbid! George S. Odiorue, author of *The Human Side of Management*, insists, "Nothing gives a man a sense of failure so often as an overdeveloped sense of perfection."

It's a mystery to many people "why" they are stuck in the procrastination trap. How does procrastination become a strong pattern of functioning, in effect take on a life of its own? It's an avoidance trap. When you avoid something that scares you, those fearful feelings and the accompanying physical symptoms often diminish or disappear. Because the behavior of avoiding or escaping was so powerful in halting what is distressing, it becomes more likely that you will use this response again when the same or similar situation presents itself. Avoidance has gained strength. Avoidance leads to more avoidance. And thus, a debilitating habit takes hold. Winston Churchill declares, "The maxim 'Nothing but perfection' may be spelled 'Paralysis.'"

Relationship problems

Relationship problems often abound in the life of the perfectionist. There are two major areas that create conflict. On one hand, upheaval can occur due to the unrealistic, intrusive expectations of the perfectionist. Others often don't agree with or live up to these standards and may harbor deep resentment because of these expectations. On the other hand, the perfectionist often has an overwhelming need to be number one in most or all endeavors, which creates a rigid, competitive lifestyle that can be poisonous to interpersonal interactions. Bill Lemley warns, "When nobody around you seems to measure up, it's time to check your yardstick."

Personal boundaries are often seriously violated by perfectionists. They usurp the rights and responsibilities that belong to another person, believing that people should change for them, follow their rules and emulate their behaviors. I've had clients related to prickly perfectionists who compare their situation to a dictator state, the despot of course being the perfectionist. Children of perfectionists are at risk for poor self-esteem, whether or not they model the behaviors and thinking of the perfectionist.

Difficulty feeling good, enjoying life and relaxing

David Burns, psychiatrist and author of *Feeling Good: The New Mood Therapy* warns, "Perfectionism becomes a badge of honor with you, playing the part of the suffering hero." Perfectionists have difficulty feeling successful and tranquil. They often experience feelings of shame, inadequacy, loneliness, sadness, frustration, guilt and disappointment. Though they may appear to have high self-esteem because they display a confidence of knowing exactly how things should be and how to make them happen, in fact the opposite -- low self-esteem -- is more generally the case.

It's difficult to enjoy yourself when even leisure activities fall into the category of "anything worth doing is worth doing right." Enjoyment, happiness and relaxation often elude them. If you're a perfectionist, an important question to ask yourself is, "Do I want to be perfect, or do I want to be happy?" The research suggests that these two are mutually exclusive entities. According to Hugh Prather, the bestselling author of *Notes to Myself,* "Perfectionism is slow death."

WHAT YOU CAN DO

If you've determined by now that you're a full-blown perfectionist, or just someone who has tendencies toward this approach to life, you need to know that you can turn this ship around. It will take effort and tenacity, but your efforts will be well worth it. Anna Quindlen contends, "The thing that is really hard and really amazing is giving up on being perfect and beginning the work of becoming yourself."

Change your misguided thinking and expectations

The perfectionist who wants to change needs to take a close look at her beliefs and expectations. To do this, start by reviewing the beliefs at the beginning of this article. Identify where your thinking is extreme. Also, determine if your perfectionism is directed at only you or at others as well.

Start by changing your belief that perfectionism is something to strive for, that it's the right way to live. Dispute this belief when the thought comes to mind. Disputing is a technique in which you attack the toxic belief by finding evidence to the contrary. Develop a conversation that you can have with yourself when the belief is influencing the decisions you make, the actions you take and your internal reactions. The last chapter of this book explains exactly how to use disputing.

Next, target the specific beliefs that are part of your particular brand of perfectionism. For example: "Mistakes and failures are shameful and therefore unacceptable," or "I must always be right and do the right thing." Construct a disputing exercise for each of your beliefs. Take them one at a time. You might find it helpful to use a quote that appeals to you as a competing, disputing response. I've sprinkled quotes throughout that may be meaningful for you. For example, I particularly like the one by David Burns: "Aim for success, not perfection. Never give up your right to be wrong, because then you will lose the ability to learn new things and move forward with your life." If you do choose a quote, have it visible in a number of places to continually remind yourself of your new, more adaptable beliefs.

Review the expectations you have of yourself and others. Use disputing for these, as well, in order to develop reasonable, achievable calculations about how things should be. For example, keep in mind that mistakes, obstacles, even failures are to be expected and are not a recipe for disaster. Understand that they are opportunities to learn and get stronger; adopt that as part of your new belief system.

Practice kindness, acceptance and self-compassion

Mark Twain maintains, "Kindness is a language which the deaf can hear and the blind can see." The strength of kindness has received much attention in Positive Psychology, and rightly so. Kindness makes people happier, helps them appreciate what they have, and brings them closer to others. Being kind to others, considering how they feel, and what choices belong to them, can be a huge step in treating others with the dignity and respect that produces deep, healthy and meaningful relationships. Be kinder and more patient. Learn to listen and have empathy. By focusing on kindness toward others, you will be able to make a significant dent into your perfectionism toward others.

The power of kindness probably surprises no one as a competing response to perfectionism. Self-kindness is about how we treat ourselves, what we expect of ourselves, what we believe about ourselves and what we say to ourselves in our internal dialogue. Unfortunately, perfectionists often treat themselves with terrible disdain. Some of their beliefs, self-talk and actions suggest disappointment and self-loathing.

Self-kindness is different from high self-esteem (HSE). Though our society has prized high self-esteem for a long time, HSE produces some negative effects such as an increase in self-absorption and the need to regard oneself as superior to others (1). Researchers have identified three components to self-kindness:

o **Self-compassion instead of self-judgment**: People who are kind to themselves are tolerant and loving toward themselves when faced with pain or failure. Self-judging people are tough and intolerant toward themselves.

o **Common humanity instead of isolation**: Common humanity is a perspective that views our own failings and feelings of inadequacy as part of the human condition shared by nearly everyone. By contrast, people who isolate tend to feel alone in their failure.

o **Emotional regulation instead of over-identification**: People who can regulate their emotions take a balanced view and keep their emotions in perspective. They neither ignore nor ruminate on elements of their lives that they dislike. By contrast, over-identified people tend to obsess and fixate on failure and view it as evidence of their personal inadequacy.

There are many wonderful benefits of self-kindness (2):

o Greater optimism, happiness and curiosity
o Reductions in anxiety, depression, anger and negative obsessing
o Reduced perfectionism and self-criticism
o Improved self-worth
o Reduction in feelings of inferiority and failure
o Less social comparison

o Feeling and being more connected to others
o Greater goal completion

Mindfulness is an important component of self-compassion. Mindfulness is a process of balancing untoward thoughts and feelings with awareness, but without focusing and perseverating on them (3).

Learn more about mindfulness

Dogen Zenji advises, "To be in harmony with the wholeness of things is not to have anxiety over imperfections." Mindfulness is a comprehensive, research-based approach that elucidates methods to bring about living in the present. The perfectionist's approach is so often a mindless one. You have so much to gain by turning mindlessness into mindfulness.

According to Jon Kabat-Zinn, mindfuness is a simple concept. Its power lies in its practice and application. Mindfulness means paying attention in a particular way: on purpose, in the present moment and non-judgmentally. This kind of attention nurtures greater awareness, clarity and acceptance of the present-moment reality. It wakes us up to the fact that our lives unfold only in moments. If we are not fully present for many of those moments, we may not only miss what is most valuable in our lives but also fail to realize the richness and the depth of our possibilities for growth and transformation (4).

Henepola Gunaratana, the Sri Lankan Buddhist monk, enumerates some of the main characteristics of mindfulness in his book, *Mindfulness in Plain English* (5):

o Mindfulness is nonjudgmental observation; the mind observes without criticism.
o Mindfulness is an impartial watchfulness; it does not try to avoid bad mental states or become possessed with good mental states.
o Mindfulness is "bare attention," that is it does not get involved with thoughts, concepts, does not get entangled by ideas, opinions, memories.

o Mindfulness is present-time awareness, the observance of what is happening right now.

o Mindfulness takes place without reference to self. Experiencing pain is merely noted as a sensation and not expressed as "I have a pain."

o Mindfulness is awareness of change; it involves the observation of experience as it flows.

o Mindfulness is observation and participation at the same time.

o Mindfulness reminds the one meditating of what he or she is supposed to be doing. If your mind should wander, mindfulness makes you aware of that.

o Mindfulness does not distort the experience. You see things as they really are.

Being in the moment deepens our connections in relationships and life. Thich Nhat Hanh, the Vietnamese Zen Buddhist monk, points out, "Life can be found only in the present moment. The past is gone, the future is not yet here, and if we do not go back to ourselves in the present moment, we cannot be in touch with life." He also tells us, "The most precious gift we can offer others is our presence. When mindfulness embraces those we love, they will bloom like flowers."

Forgiveness and acceptance of yourself and others

An Egyptian proverb declares, "A beautiful thing is never perfect." Accepting others and yourself for who you are, warts and all, is an approach that can free you from the shackles of perfectionism. Acceptance and forgiveness mean that you accept that flaws and missteps are part of being human, part of an individual's uniqueness and part of a person's journey. It's a kind and smart thing to do if you want to have healthy relationships.

Anatole France says, "I cling to my imperfection as the very essence of my being." If you view imperfections as part of a person's uniqueness, those imperfections take on a whole new meaning. Leonard Cohen, the Canadian singer-songwriter, poet and novelist, encourages us to find this meaning:

"Ring the bells that still can ring
Forget your perfect offering.
There is a crack in everything,
That's how the light gets in."

Give yourself permission to be imperfect and to make mistakes; learn to see the humor in your mistakes. See the imperfections of yourself and others as contributing to individuality.

Learn about procrastination and plan an anti-avoidance approach

Understand that procrastination is a form of avoidance. The perfectionist avoids finishing a project because of her fear it will lead to an evaluation of performance by herself or by someone else. To conquer this fear, one needs to become desensitized to it, which involves a step-by-step process. Start with the least anxiety-producing situation in which you're procrastinating. When you've managed that one, you move on to the next one that's least anxiety producing, and so on. In the last chapter there's a complete description of how to go about doing this. The perfectionist avoids criticism. This is one of the beliefs that will need to be changed. One must look at constructive criticism as positive and not catastrophic.

Face all your fears

Ralph Waldo Emerson contends, "Fear defeats more people than any one thing in the world." Whatever you fear and give in to restricts your choices and abilities in life. It owns you. Figure out what fears lurk behind your perfectionism and face them directly. Desensitization, one of the techniques discussed in the last chapter, can be utilized to manage the fears that are holding you back. If this is too difficult to do alone, talk to a psychologist or other health care professional

Develop a sense of humor about yourself

Inject a humorous approach to your life and goals. So many things in life just aren't that serious or important, but the perfectionist has a faulty system of labeling practically everything as serious. She definitely takes herself too seriously. Start to think in terms of a one to ten rating system in which one indicates "not serious at all" and ten indicates "very serious." Keep in mind that being able to laugh at yourself is a wonderful and freeing experience. Resign as CEO of the universe; it will be a relief for you and others.

Set realistic, achievable goals

Get to know what you really want out of your life. You may want to create a "Bucket List." Just as in the movie by the same name, this is a list of those things that really matter to you. Unleash that part of the brain that loves to dream in order to help you find what would bring joy and meaning to your life. Be sure to congratulate yourself when you complete any part of your goal. Look at life and your goals as a journey, not as a destination. Be realistic and flexible in terms of the time required to complete your goals. Adopt a flexible approach in goal setting and goal attainment. Reality often dictates changes in direction along the way.

You can be excellent, but not perfect, at some chosen goals, and just plain mediocre at others that don't matter much at all. Make the decision to be selective about which endeavors merit your finest efforts, and then plan to revel in your accomplishments -- even the ones that may fall short of the mark.

Adopt an optimistic attitude

Elbert Hubbard believes, "Optimism is a kind of heart stimulant -- the digitalis of failure." When something bad happens or you make a mistake or fail at an endeavor, adopt an optimistic attitude. When in the midst of adversity, the optimist doesn't take it personally, doesn't think it's permanent and doesn't allow the mishap to affect unrelated parts of her life. The pessimist does the exact opposite.

1.Neff, K. D., and Vonk, R. (2009). "Self-Compassion Versus Global Self-Esteem: Two Different Ways of Relating to Oneself." Journal of Personality, 77(1), 23-50.

2. Safigan, S. (2010) "Self-Kindness: A Healthier Alternative to Self-Esteem" Positive Psychology News Daily

3. Neff, K. D. and Lamb, L. M. (2009) "Self-Compassion" The Encyclopedia of Positive Psychology

4. Kabat-Zinn (1994) Wherever You Go, There You Are: Mindfulness Meditation Everyday Life

5. Guarantana, H. (1993) Mindfulness in Plain English

Chapter 8
STUCK IN THE VICTIM ROLE?

"Definition of a victim: a person to whom life happens."
Peter McWilliams

The VICTIM BELIEF: My problems are caused by others or by circumstances

This belief is a problem if you tell yourself:

o I am a victim
o I need others to take care of me because of my compromised state
o I need someone to blame to avoid feelings of guilt or shame; it's terrible to have made a mistake or failed at something
o Some things are so overwhelming, I have to figure who's responsible so I can feel okay
o I don't believe I have to take responsibility for my behavior
o I am helpless in making my life as I would like it to be
o I am helpless in getting beyond the abuse that has occurred in my life
o I am wounded and can't get beyond the hurt
o I have been treated unfairly
o Life should be fair
o Because I have been a victim, I can avoid situations that scare me or make me uncomfortable
o When others feel sorry for me, I get more attention and more help
o I should resent how I've been treated for a long time
o Only someone who is a bad person would hurt me; bad people should be punished

Casting yourself in the role of the victim in your inner world and in your public persona is a straight shot to pain, disappointment and ineffectiveness. This misguided approach marginalizes your capacity to live a fruitful, powerful and rewarding existence. It restricts your options, blocks your ability to make your goals and dreams come true, and can weaken your confidence in yourself. Believing you are a victim and acting like one can have seriously negative effects on your relationships. People who immerse themselves in the victim role are not much fun to be around!

Martin Seligman, the world-renowned Positive Psychologist, explains that "victimology" -- blaming our problems on other people and circumstances -- is directly related to the concept of "learned helplessness." Learned helplessness, often a major factor in depression, is a well-documented phenomenon in which an individual does not believe that his/her actions matter in terms of how things turn out. The victim believes that events and circumstances are controlled by external forces rather than by his choices and actions.

Another manifestation of the victim mentality is self-pity. John Gardner tells us, "Self-pity is easily the most destructive of the non-pharmaceutical narcotics; it is addictive, gives momentary pleasure and separates the victim from reality." Quite honestly, self-pity is a mindset that brings nothing but misery and dysfunction. It takes you out of the driver's seat and puts you in the trunk. Most of us feel a degree of self-pity from time to time. But the sooner we put it behind us, the sooner we get back to orchestrating our own life, and the sooner we can resume being a better partner, relative, friend and coworker. The Scottish philosopher Dr. Megan Reik explains, "There are few human emotions as warm, comforting and enveloping as self-pity. And nothing is more corrosive and destructive. There is only one answer; turn away from it and move on."

How this happens

How do people fall prey to the victim role? I can think of several possible ways. Some people feel helpless for one reason or another, and this helplessness can produce a great deal of anxiety. The anxious person often looks for some way to quell the uncomfortable feelings. Finding another to blame may, in the victim's mind, relieve him of the responsibility, blunting how disappointed he is in himself. This may reduce the anxiety to some degree. In a maladjusted way, playing the victim may increase a person's feeling of control.

92

Some people learned to use this as a coping mechanism early on, perhaps due to the ways in which they were parented. The parent may have made excuses for the child, preventing the child from learning to take responsibility for his own behavior. One or both parents may have modeled the blaming approach in handling mistakes, failures and misfortunes. There may be increased attention from others who feel sorry for the self-anointed victim. Or feeling like a victim might serve as an excuse to avoid some circumstance that evokes fear or that's regarded as distasteful. Or perhaps, ensconcing oneself in this role is a way to feel special. Whatever the reason or the way this came about, you can be sure it does not serve you well.

Are you are caught in this trap? If so, extricating yourself might just be one of the healthiest changes you'll ever make. It's not only your right, but more importantly your responsibility, to decide if the victim role serves you or imprisons you. In my experience as a psychologist, the victim role is a form of psychological paralysis. No matter who or what has "done you wrong," it will not bring you psychological health and self-confidence to espouse the victim mentality. By definition, a victim is one who has been injured, destroyed, tricked, duped or given a raw deal; and even if you have experienced something devastating and/or patently unfair, this approach is absolutely not a healthy solution.

Victims are often poisoned by self-denigration and the resentment of others. If you've been seriously abused and cannot get past your injuries, I would recommend you seek professional help. This can be tough territory to go alone. Otherwise, get past it by looking at it from the power point. Power comes from letting go of the blame and resentment and taking responsibility for all aspects of your life.

But I have a right to feel victimized!

Even though you may feel strongly that you've been victimized and that this victimization must be rectified to your satisfaction, by continuing to focus on what happened and who or what was to blame, your energy is being wasted. Outside forces control your life.

There's something very important for the person beset by the victim mentality to get straight: you have a choice about how you view difficulties. You get to choose what you think, what you believe and what you expect to happen. You get to decide if an event or a person has control over your life or if you do. It's your decision whether or not to take responsibility for your actions. If you believe that you're entitled to feel victimized when something bad happens to you, you may want to make a reality check -- try a more objective look at how things really work and do a cost/benefit analysis.

Bad things happen to everyone. Failures, mistakes, obstacles, disappointments, and so on occur frequently. Really bad things happen to many people. Loved ones die. Serious physical and mental illness plagues us or someone close to us. Natural disasters such as fires, floods, tornadoes and hurricanes bring horror into many lives. Some of us are terrorized by people who hate us.

Some of us lose jobs, have serious marital problems or raise children who manifest heartbreaking difficulties. Many fail to achieve important goals at one time or another, often repeatedly. Some of us are abused as children or adults. Many of us grow up in poverty or live our adult lives in poverty. Some know the hell of war or captivity. Most people experience times when numerous changes and difficulties besiege us all at once. These realities cross all cultures and walks of life. We have little or no control over the occurrence of the more traumatic events and serious problems.

But we do have a choice about how we perceive, react to and utilize these situations. Some people allow trouble of any kind to stop them in their tracks. Some people are overwhelmed by very stressful events to the point of being paralyzed, while others react with a diminished ability to cope and enjoy life. Then there are individuals with a skill set that enables them to return to pre-difficulty functioning, or even more amazingly, to a state of greater strength, wisdom, commitment and connection to life.

Understanding and accepting that bad things happen to everyone is an important step in becoming resilient, to relieving yourself of the burden of being stuck with the belief that you're a victim. People

who are resilient, who handle trouble adroitly, are not lucky – they're skilled. They possess beliefs and behaviors that are adaptable and proactive. People without the skills are often at the mercy of life's mishaps and are susceptible to responses of anguish and despair that can last a very long time. Fortunately for them, becoming more resilient is certainly achievable.

If you accept that trouble just happens and give up looking for a scapegoat, you will be less likely to react in shock and awe when unwanted disturbances turn your world upside down. You'll be in a better position to formulate an effective approach for these times -- a plan that helps you regain the forward movement of your vision and dreams. You'll be able to divest yourself of your role as one of life's victims -- and your life will be your own. Cicero contends, "It's foolish to tear ones hair in grief, as though sorrow would be made less by baldness."

Theodor Geisel (aka, Dr. Seuss), in a pep talk on negotiating the journey of life with its slings and arrows, conveys the message best:

But on you will go though the weather be foul
On you will go though your enemies prowl…
On and on you'll hike and I know you'll hike far
And face up to your problems wherever you are…
So be sure when you step, step with care and great tact
And remember that Life's a Great Balancing Act.
And will you succeed?
Yes, you will indeed!
(98 and 3/4 percent guaranteed.)

Are you plagued by the victim mindset?

The first step in tackling the craziness of the victim belief is to assess how it manifests in your life and how it impacts your ability to be self-reliant. You might find it helpful to answer each of the following questions to get a better idea of what part the victim role plays in your life:

o When did you start feeling like a victim?

o What happened that precipitated your feeling like a victim?

o Who or what do you think is responsible for your victimization?

o Why do you believe that what happened had such a strong impact on your functioning?

o Describe your feelings of victimization. Do you feel angry, scared, frustrated, etc? How do these feelings restrict your options in life?

o How much time and energy do you devote to this role of being a victim? Do you talk on and on to others about your difficulties? Do you think about the unfairness of what has happened often? Does it dominate how you live your life?

o Do you believe in general that your problems are caused by others or by circumstances?

o Do you believe that you are helpless in overcoming the abuse or victimization that has occurred or continues to occur?

o Do you believe that you are helpless in making your life as you'd like it to be?

o Do you believe that your decisions and actions have little or no effect on the way things turn out for you?

o Do you believe that you are unable to get beyond the hurt?

o Do you believe that you need others to take care of you because of what happened?

o Do you think a lot about how people or life have treated you unfairly? Do you believe life "should be fair?"

o Do you feel entitled to feel resentful? Do you believe that you're powerless to stop your feelings of resentment?

o Do you believe that others should feel sorry for you?

o Does being in the victim role make you feel special?

o Do you expect less of yourself because of what has happened? Do you expect others to be more understanding and less demanding because you've been victimized?

o Do you believe you should punish the person who did this to you?

o Do you believe that because you have been victimized it's acceptable to avoid setting goals, and making decisions that are uncomfortable?

o Do you believe you're responsible for what happens to you?

o Do you believe that your reality is a function of your thoughts and actions?

o Do you think of people as pernicious because of how they've behaved toward you?

Changing from victim to victor

For people caught up in the victim mentality, I have very good news: you can free yourself from this self-imposed, self-defeating, depressing approach to life. Changing your attitude from victim to victor will go a long way in helping you take control of what is really your right and responsibility -- *your life!* You need to trust in your own power to make your life and future better. Develop positive beliefs, expectations, choices and strategies. Accept that you're the one who's responsible for your life. According to an unknown author, "If you kicked the person in the pants responsible for most of your trouble, you wouldn't sit for a month."

Learn how to dispute the beliefs and expectations that make you feel helpless

The victim role is yet another example of thoughts and beliefs gone amok. You get to decide if an event or a person has control over your life or if you do. Identify the beliefs and expectations you may have that promote feelings of helplessness. Dedicate your efforts to disputing beliefs and expectations that keep you trapped in the victim role. The last chapter will help you do this effectively.

Make a decision to change your view of yourself as a victim

By looking for the opportunities in the midst of difficulty, you change your focus from helplessness to self-reliance and hope. Appreciate what's working in your life and consider what you can do to move things forward. Pay attention to the qualities and strengths in each of the people in your world instead of blaming them or making them responsible for your problems. Start using the vocabulary of someone who considers himself to be the architect of his life.

One way to usher in positive change is to develop a "self-talk" that's like a mentor or an admired, trusted friend. In your own voice, conduct internal conversations similar to those you'd have with someone who encourages you and sees you as a profound work in progress. Just as a mentor or friend would question and dispute your irrational beliefs about yourself or would challenge you on destructive criticism, do the same. Just as the mentor or friend would reinforce your positive behaviors and thinking, so should you.

Some people find it helpful in developing this voice to first utilize the "internal guide," a technique in which you choose a mentor with whom you have ongoing conversations. This guide is wise and cares about you. It can be someone you know, have known or would like to know because of your admiration and respect for his or her attitude toward life. This is a method to recalibrate your thinking process. Really imagine you're talking to this person and receiving suggestions and sage advice that compete with any garbage you throw at yourself or others. Some of my clients have successfully used the "internal guide" as an ongoing strategy in their quest to become more powerful on their own behalf.

Say "no way" to the blame game

Blame is a huge detour from the path of power. It seriously restricts an individual's ability to change. As Wayne Dyer contends, "All blame is a waste of time. No matter how much fault you find with another, and regardless of how much you blame him, it will not change you. The only thing blame does is keep the focus off you when you are looking for external reasons to explain your unhappiness or frustration. You may succeed in making another feel guilty about something, but you won't succeed in changing whatever it is about you that's making you unhappy."

Decide that you will dispute any self-talk that identifies another as the cause of your problems. Have the conversation with yourself about what you have control over and what you do not. Use your energy in the service of the positive changes you can target. A really potent way to replace blaming others is to change your focus to gratitude -- gratitude for your blessings and for the good things about others. Showing gratitude is a wonderful way to increase your happiness, improve your relationships and enable you to be the "master of your fate."

Commit to removing resentment from your life

Resentment is something that occurs when you blame others or the world for your problems or deficits in life. It's an ongoing attenuation of your energy and a huge deterrent to living a productive and happy life. Resentment means trouble for you and for those with whom you come in contact. Friedrich Nietzsche maintains, "Nothing on earth consumes a man more quickly than the passion of resentment."

Resentment is something that rarely gets resolved unless one decides to just let it go. When you think about it, the person who harbors resentment really has appointed himself the center of the universe. It's a selfish and insidious approach to life. As Ann Landers says, "Resentment is letting someone you hate live rent-free in your head."

Refuse to make excuses or use alibis

Victims often become experts at using excuses and alibis. Excuses and alibis lead you down a seductive and thorny path to impotence. The person who sees himself as a victim often learns to make excuses for the things he chooses not to do. In his mind he's concluded that he's entitled to use this method because of his compromised state for which, of course, someone else is responsible. Excuses and alibis are tools of avoidance. You talk yourself out of facing the difficult, the fearful, the unknown, the boring; you grant yourself a pass citing specific reasons, and often quite persuasively so. The excuse/alibi mentality involves avoidance, which so often becomes addictive. When you avoid something negative, you feel momentarily better, and the excuse/alibi gets reinforced. The likelihood of the avoidance occurring again increases, sometimes markedly.

Eric Hoffer enlightens us about alibis when he tells us, "There are many who find a good alibi far more attractive than an achievement. For an achievement does not settle anything permanently. We still have to prove that we are as good today as we were yesterday. But when we have a valid alibi for not achieving anything, we are fixed, so to speak, for life. Moreover, when we have an alibi for not writing a book and not painting a picture and so on, we have an alibi for not writing the greatest book and not painting the greatest picture. Small wonder that the effort expended and the punishment endured in obtaining a good alibi often exceed the effort and grief requisite for the attainment of a most marked achievement."

Learn how to manage anxiety and depression

People who are ensnared in the victim role often suffer from anxiety and depression. While emancipating yourself from this particular set of irrational beliefs will help you reduce both anxiety and depression, there are other skills that can be learned to manage these debilitating afflictions. An excellent book to help with depression is *Feeling Good: the New Mood Therapy* (1999) by David Burns. For help with anxiety, I would recommend: *The Anxiety and Phobia Workbook* (2005) by Edmund Bourne.

Accept that others make mistakes and learn forgiveness

I've met a number of people who really believe that because someone hurt them, even when it might have been unwittingly, that person should be regarded as malignant and should suffer some punishment. People are not bad because they're different from you. People are not without faults. That includes you. They make mistakes, sometimes again and again. We hurt others and others hurt us. Are there some people who have done heinous acts? Yes, of course. Even in these extreme cases, however, it does not serve us well to obsess about or promote the demise of another human being. Always ask yourself, "does a belief system or a course of action bring positive energy to your life or does it deplete it?" Focusing on anger and revenge debilitates the raging victim. Lewis B. Smedes contends, "To forgive is to set a prisoner free and discover that the prisoner was you."

Forgiveness is one of the 24 character strengths researched in the field of Positive Psychology. According to Michael McCullough, a researcher at the University of Miami, forgiving is a choice we have that avails us to new possibilities in relationships (http://www.psy.miami.edu/faculty/mmccullough/). Marianne Williamson concludes, "Forgiveness is the choice to see people as they are now. When we are angry at people, we are angry because of something they said or did before this moment. But what people said or did is not who they are. Relationships are reborn as we let go perceptions of our brother's past. By bringing the past into the present, we create a future just like the past. By letting the past go, we make room for miracles."

Chapter 9
CHANGING CRAZY BELIEFS -- *The Nuts and Bolts*

After reading the chapter on each belief, go back and spend some time reviewing the sub beliefs. Write down any sub beliefs that apply to you consistently and frequently. Try to identify thoughts that go along with each sub belief. For example, if one sub belief is, "I need to be perfect and successful in everything I do," then identify the thoughts and images that are connected, such as "I can't hand in my paper to the professor until every word is perfect," or "I don't want to run the marathon because I might not win." Or you may conjure up an image of falling down in the race and being mortified.

One way to compile this information is to write down all types of associated thoughts, images, beliefs, perceptions, etc. in a notebook as they occur. For one week, keep the notebook accessible so that you're able to perform a comprehensive assessment. Some cognitions will be more obvious to you than others. Keep track of the frequency of each cognition, the intensity of your response to it (one to ten, ten being most intense), how long each lasts and at what time it occurred. Note if there is a specific trigger for that thought. This is a lot of work, but it gets much easier as you get the hang of it.

Once you've accomplished this, take the thematic belief, the sub beliefs and the thoughts, images, etc. that accompany them, and apply four main techniques: Diaphragmatic Breathing, Thought Stopping, Disputing and Systematic Desensitization (specifically for The Fear Belief). Diaphragmatic breathing has a twofold purpose. First, it's a very effective way to reduce stress and anxiety, which makes the process of modifying your beliefs less overwhelming. Second, as a major component of the Self-Control Triad (Thought Stopping) and Systematic Desensitization, it's best to become adroit at deep breathing in advance of learning these techniques. The Self-Control Triad helps you reduce the frequency, intensity and duration of the troubling cognitions, while Disputing helps you challenge and change the content of the beliefs from unreasonable and debilitating to reasonable and energizing. These are companion techniques that are very powerful when applied consistently and firmly. Systematic Desensitization is a procedure to help you face your fears.

Diaphragmatic breathing

It's hard to emphasize enough the importance of breathing in your quest to manage the stress response and take control of your life. Your choice is: deep abdominal breathing or shallow chest breathing. The diaphragm, which is under the lungs and just above the abdomen, is the most efficient breathing muscle and is connected to the relaxed nervous system -- the parasympathetic nervous system (PNS). Abdominal breathing is deep and slow, promoting mental concentration, decreased body tension and anxiety, and a greater supply of oxygen to the brain.

Chest breathing is shallow and rapid. The chest muscles are in a state of tension. This type of breathing is connected to the stress nervous system -- the sympathetic nervous system (SNS) -- with all its symptoms, including increased heart rate and blood pressure, decreased mental acuity and concentration, and elevated anxiety levels. Some chest breathers are prone to hyperventilation, which is a very uncomfortable state.

Most people don't have a clue about their breathing patterns but discover that breathing abdominally makes a huge difference in stress levels and produces an overall sense of personal control. Abdominal breathing is easy to learn and maintain. If you watch a baby lying on his back you'll notice his abdomen moving up and down with little or no movement in the chest area. The baby didn't have to learn to do this because it's a built-in response. But as people experience stress, they often shift to shallow breathing, which can become a chronic state. This is your chance to return to the relaxed breathing that once came so naturally. Now for the steps:

STEP 1

Find a comfortable, quiet place, preferably lying on a bed, recliner or on a blanket on the floor. Choose a spot where you won't be disturbed for the next 10 minutes.

STEP 2

Close your eyes. Put your right hand over your chest and your left hand over your abdomen in the area of your belly button. Keep these hands in place for the duration of the exercise. This is how you'll be able to tell where you're breathing.

STEP 3

Take several deep breaths paying attention to which hand is moving. If your right hand is moving, you're chest breathing; if your left hand is moving, you're abdominally breathing. You may find that both hands are moving. The goal is to have only the left hand moving when you inhale.

STEP 4

Imagine that you have a red balloon in your abdomen underneath your belly button and that there's a tube extending from your chest to the opening of the balloon where the tube is attached. Inhale through your nose, sending the air straight down the tube (no movement in the chest) and to the balloon, blowing it up like a child's party balloon. Pause for three seconds, and then exhale, sending the air back up the tube and out your nose or mouth, whichever is more comfortable for you.

STEP 5

Wait three seconds before inhaling again. Inhale through the nose and direct the air to inflate the red balloon. Keep the balloon inflated for three seconds and then exhale slowly, waiting three seconds before the next breath. Be aware of your hand positions and where the breathing movement is occurring on the inhale. Repeat this pattern for 10 minutes. Do this twice a day.

STEP 6

After you've practiced this for several days and are confident that you're breathing abdominally during the exercise, check your breathing throughout the day in a variety of circumstances and locations to see if you're chest or belly breathing. For example, check yourself while you're reading, walking, cooking dinner or working. If your breathing is shallow, imagine the red balloon and shift the breathing to your abdomen. Your goal is to generalize your abdominal breathing so it becomes a habit that can serve you most if not all the time. Continue to check this frequently.

STEP 7

The image of the red balloon that you've practiced and used in general is a learned image that can help you when you're feeling stressed or anxious. Whether you're in the middle of the stress situation or are anticipating some stressful circumstance, just imagine the red balloon and do as much of the abdominal breathing exercise as you can wherever you are.

STEP 8

Continue practicing the 10 minute breathing exercise every day or at least several times a week. Practicing often reduces the stress response in general and keeps you focused on maintaining abdominal breathing.

Thought stopping

"Thought Stopping" was introduced by Bain in his 1928 book, *Thought Control in Everyday Life.* Joseph Wolpe and others in the field of behavior therapy applied Thought Stopping as a technique to diminish anxiety and obsessive thoughts. By using Thought Stopping, an individual can control what goes on in the cognitive domain. Since negative thoughts are often antecedents to negative emotions, when you control these thoughts you can change emotional responses as well. Knowing how to exert control makes all the difference. Your thoughts are learned and have gained strength by repetition; by refusing in a concerted, consistent and tenacious way to allow certain thoughts to appear, by distracting your focus from negative thoughts, images and beliefs and turning to positive, motivating cognitions or activities, you can reshape your mental landscape.

Distraction methods are very effective ways to shrink the number, strength and amount of time you spend involved with beliefs and thoughts that cause you nothing but trouble. Distraction and Disputing work well together. Distraction reduces the occurrence of the thinking and then disputing questions the veracity and usefulness of the claims that remain. For example, if you keep focusing on how fat you are, distraction is useful in diminishing the number of times you say that to yourself in a given day; it may also reduce the strength of the response you have to that particular thought/belief. Disputing is then used to question the accuracy and usefulness of your belief and the advisability of considering that this is so important to you.

Distraction is about saying "no" to one response and being ready to replace it with another, more adaptive response. This can be done by directly addressing the thoughts in your head or by opting for a competing external activity. The internal exercise I'm going to discuss is one that many of my clients rave about: The Self-Control Triad. The external approach involves switching to an activity that competes with thinking, such as playing a sport, watching an engrossing or very funny movie, singing a silly song, playing a video game, engaging in a hobby that holds your attention. The external distractions are often less accessible than the internal one which is available to you whenever you need it and wherever you are.

The Self-Control Triad

The Self-Control Triad is a very effective technique that was developed in the early 1980's by Joseph R. Cautela, my mentor at Boston College. The Self-Control Triad has three major parts: thought stopping, abdominal breathing and positive imagery. The idea is to strongly say *STOP!* to a negative thought, belief, expectation, etc.; then switch to abdominal breathing to distract and relax you; and finally to replace the unwanted cognition with one that's positive and competes with the undesirable one. The steps to using the triad to your advantage are as follows:

106

Thought stopping

The *STOP!* has to be loud, clear and forceful -- something that comes with a lot of practice. To start the practice, make sure you're in a comfortable place where no one will disturb you. Close your eyes and yell *STOP!* in your head. Try to make it as loud as possible as if you are hearing a rock band at full volume. Try to make it as forceful as if you saw a child or dog running into the street with a car coming and your voice alone could save them. Measure both the loudness and the force on a one to 10 scale, with 10 being the highest. Don't be discouraged if you're at the low end on both as you begin this new learning process. Practice this again and again. If you continue to have difficulty making the *STOP!* loud and strong, find a method to record yourself yelling *STOP!* out loud. Listen to the recording, then close your eyes and try to replicate your yell. Continue to do this until the loudness and strength are above an eight.

Some people have much better visual than auditory imagery. If this is true for you, use the image of a stop sign or a stop light along with the auditory imagery or just by itself. But keep in mind the visual images also need to be strong enough to compete with your strongest negative cognitions.

When the loudness and force are eight or above in your estimation, you're ready to try it on an actual negative thought. Choose a specific thought from your inventory that's not above 6 on the intensity of response rating. With your eyes closed, focus on that thought; make it as clear and as daunting as you can. Then yell *STOP!* inside your head until the thought is no longer present. Repeat this procedure five times.

Abdominal breathing

I've discussed abdominal breathing above. Review this material and practice this now for five minutes. While you're relaxed, close your eyes, think the negative thought, thought stop, and then switch to deep breathing. If the thought should come back on its own, thought stop, then breathe. Practice this sequence for five trials.

Imagery

What images or thoughts bring you strength, energy and joy? Spend some time thinking of the many possibilities. These can be beautiful places you've been, experiences you've had or would like to have, eating your favorite food, laughing with your friends, succeeding at your fondest goal, remembering all the good things about yourself, listening to music, and so on. Be sure your image does not remind you of something that will evoke negative feelings. For example, if you choose the image of walking on the beach, but that's where a boyfriend broke up with you, this probably isn't a good choice.

You'll need to have many positive images available in your repertoire because if you overuse one it loses its strength to compete with the negative belief or thought. So variety is very important in this exercise. Dr. Cautela had one image that he used for himself that definitely brought a smile to my face. He imagined he was a crew member (a psychologist, of course) on Star Trek! So use your imagination.

The effectiveness of these images or thoughts will very much depend on two variables which you need to measure on the one to 10 scale: clarity of the image, and how reinforcing the image is to you at this time. These positive images or thoughts must be high-powered to compete with cognitions that have occupied so much time in your head. Spend time on one specific image, getting the clarity and reinforcement to an eight or above. This can take practice, so be patient.

Putting it all together

Thought>Thought Stop>Breathe>Image

Think about the belief, thought or image that you wish to change. Make sure it's as clear and as strong as you can get it. Thought stop until the thought or image is gone. Deep breathe and then think the

108

positive thought or image. Take time to enjoy the pleasure of this. If the negative image returns, thought stop and continue the whole sequence again. Do this sequence 10 times with 30 seconds between each trial.

Other instructions and information

o Practice two sessions per day, 10 triads per session.
o One session is with your eyes closed and one with them open. This is because you will need to use the triad throughout your day sometimes when your eyes need to be open.
o Choose three positive images in the morning: one for each session and one to use on thoughts that come up outside of sessions.
o If at any time during the day you experience the negative thought you've been practicing on or other cognitions that are problematic, use the triad with your chosen positive image immediately.
o Practice on thoughts that you really want to get rid of. The practice session can reduce the power of the negative cognition. And vary the negative beliefs you're targeting.

Disputing

Robust research has shown that disputing is a very effective tool in your quest to control your inner world. Disputing is arguing with disturbing beliefs, thoughts and assumptions. It's about changing your interpretation and thus the consequent reactions you have to the adverse circumstances. The optimal change involves finding interpretations that designate the problem as not permanent, personal or pervasive. Harmful beliefs often predict that the consequences that have occurred or will occur are going to last forever, are a result of some inadequacy of yours, and that the negative effects will spread to other parts of your life. The ultimate message is that you are helpless, that nothing you do will make a difference. How demotivating and discouraging! When one is disputing problematic thematic beliefs, sub beliefs, thoughts, etc., the object is to find alternative explanations, evidence or interpretations that are changeable and don't render you feeling incapacitated.

Disputing as represented by "ABCDE" model:

A = Adversity: the trigger or antecedent to your negative belief. You need to take a close look at what elements are evoking the problematic beliefs. Example: You don't get the job for which you interviewed at the Boston law firm.

B = Belief: disturbing belief that automatically occurs in conjunction with the adversity. Example: "I am a failure and may never get a job. What made me think I could work for a law firm as prestigious as this? What an idiot I am."

C = Consequences: the usual consequences resulting from this belief. Example: You feel deflated, disappointed, ashamed and scared.

D = Disputation: the argument disputing the erroneous belief. Example: It often takes more than one interview to get hired. You remind yourself that you've had many other jobs at which you excelled, that you've had many professors who praised your accomplishments. You remind yourself of the reality that most new law school graduates have to interview with a number of firms before getting an offer. Your focus is on what you can change.

E = Energy: the energy that occurs when one disputes successfully. Example: You feel much better. You're optimistic that you can work somewhere that will be a great step in your career. You renew your search for other possibilities.

Four ways to dispute: a disputing example

"Judy" is a 40-year-old woman, married with three children. She has always wanted to go to college and now is doing so after being a stay-at-home mom. She's been experiencing a lot of self-doubt and fearful feelings about this newest challenge. Her ultimate goal is to become a paralegal and work for a prestigious law firm. She was so excited starting her first paralegal classes.

Adversity: The results of her first two exams were a B and a C, and she was devastated.

Beliefs (what she said to herself):

o I must be one of the dumbest people in the class
o What made me think I could keep up with these younger students?
o Maybe I should just quit before I embarrass myself further
o What law firm is going to hire someone my age?
o I must have been crazy to think I could pull this off.
o Things are only going to get tougher in the courses after this

Consequences: Judy felt helpless, afraid, humiliated and defeated

Disputation: four specific approaches

Evidence: find evidence to counter pessimistic beliefs. Does a B or a C on the first two tests mean Judy's the dumbest person in the class? She could find out what other students got for test scores. She could ask the professor where her scores placed her in the class. She might want to ask students who had taken the course before about the professor's grading practices. She should consider that her final grade will certainly include more tests, a paper and a final exam.

Find alternative explanations for pessimistic beliefs. Perhaps Judy didn't study hard enough for the tests, or the tests were especially difficult, or maybe she was feeling under the weather. Why latch on to most insidious explanation? Scan for all possible causes for adversity, then focus on what is changeable, specific, non-personal. Example: I didn't spend enough time studying. Next time I'll spend more (changeable). This exam was difficult (specific). The professor grades unfairly (non-personal).

Explore the implications of pessimistic beliefs: sometimes the facts you're considering are accurate. What then? One technique is "decastrophizing" -- even if Judy's belief is correct, what are its implications? Judy was older. What does that imply? It doesn't mean she's not as smart or that no one would want to hire her. She needs to ask herself how likely it is that the drastic implications she's imagined are actually probable. How likely is it that a B and a C indicate that no one will ever hire Judy?

<u>Examine the usefulness of these beliefs</u>: some beliefs are not helpful to us even if there's some truth to them. For example, holding the belief that the world should always be fair may cause more grief than it's worth. It's more useful to spend your energy in more productive ways.

Systematic Desensitization

"Fears are educated into us and can, if we wish, be educated out."
Karl Menninger

"Systematic Desensitization," also known as exposure therapy, is a highly effective method for managing fear and/or anxiety reactions to events, situations, persons or things. Joseph Wolpe, the South African psychiatrist, developed this procedure in the 1950's. Based on the classical conditioning model, this intervention is an effective treatment for phobias and anxiety disorders as well as those fear responses that don't meet the criteria for a clinical diagnosis.

Sensitization is the learning process in which anxiety/stress symptoms become associated with a given stimulus, often a neutral one, for which there is no basis for the fear. Desensitization is the unlearning of that association. When a person experiences the stress response, a common reaction is to avoid the situation that evokes fear or anxiety.

Desensitization is a step by step method for approaching fear stimuli without overwhelming you. Systematic Desensitization involves three major components: a hierarchy of anxiety-provoking situations or stimuli, the ability to generate a state of relaxation, and exercises where you pair the fear stimulus with the relaxed state. This can be done via imagery or *in vivo* (i.e., "in the actual situation").

This approach works because relaxation competes with anxiety; when you're relaxed, you're not anxious. By pairing relaxation with whatever scares you, the association with the stimulus changes from fear to calm. The number of pairings for a successful outcome varies from person to person and from situation to situation. It's important to time the pairings closely together, particularly for in vivo; if they're too far apart, the fear can regain strength.

Imagery and in vivo desensitization

In both types of desensitization, feared stimuli are arranged on a hierarchy. The exercises start with the stimulus or situation that evokes the least anxiety; in imagery, this is done by simply imagining the stimulus, and in vivo, this is done in the actual situation. When this stimulus no longer leads to an anxiety response because of repeated pairings with a relaxed state, the next one on the hierarchy is then targeted and the same procedure is followed.

Imagery Desensitization offers a number of advantages: it can be quite effective as a sole treatment; it's a way to prepare you to approach the actual situations with less discomfort; it's helpful in reducing anticipatory anxiety; and it's generally more accessible than some actual situations. For example, if you're afraid of flying, being on an airplane every day for two weeks may not be practical. In Vivo Desensitization, when done properly, is a very potent technique. I've found that using both types is especially helpful to many people.

The steps

First, develop a hierarchy for both types of desensitization. This hierarchy is based on "Subjective Units of Distress" (SUDS). Your job is to list the fearful parts of what's being avoided. Then you rate them on a one to 10 scale according to how much subjective anxiety they elicit. Consider the emotional, physical and behavioral symptoms you experience when faced with a given stimulus. This is the Subjective Units of Distress scale that's often used:

1 to 10 Scale / Subjective Distress
1 to 2 / Low Anxiety
3 to 4 / Medium Low Anxiety
5 to 6 / Medium Anxiety

7 to 8 / Medium High Anxiety
9 to 10 / High Anxiety

Actually imagine and feel your response to each facet of your fear and then assign the number that most closely approximates your subjective distress. Describe as fully as you can the specific situation. For example, if you're trying to desensitize to dogs, one situation might involve a small dog on a leash 50 yards away in an open field = SUDS of 4. What are the elements that make one situation more fearful than another? This assessment is very important, so spend some time really figuring out the variables.

The hierarchy should have as many as 15 situations, ranging in the intensity of anxiety from low to high. Then arrange them in order according to the SUDS rating, starting with the least anxiety evoking, then the next and so on. This sequence may not correspond to how the events would occur chronologically. For example, if you're afraid of flying, a lower SUDS item might be eating lunch at the airport, while a higher one might be making reservations for the dreaded flight.

The role of relaxation

To bring about a relaxed state you actually have a number of choices. These include: Progressive Muscle Relaxation, The Relaxation Response (a form of meditation), Abdominal Breathing and Imagery Relaxation. Choose the method that's best for you. Before starting each exercise, find a place where you won't be disturbed, then spend five to 10 minutes becoming deeply relaxed. I've included instructions for Abdominal (diaphragmatic) Breathing at the beginning of this chapter.

Putting Desensitization to Work: Pairing the fear stimulus with your state of relaxation

Imagery desensitization

Imagine yourself in the situation; *really be there*. Be aware of all the elements that contribute to your distress. The vividness of your imagery is very important. Maintain this imagery for several minutes. Intermittently, while you're visualizing the fear stimulus, take some deep abdominal breaths. If your anxiety exceeds a 4 rating after minute or two, return to your relaxation exercise or discontinue the imagery until your next planned session. After several minutes of visualizing the target, take a break, relax, and then do it again. When the targeted stimulus on which you're working no longer evokes anxiety, you're ready to move on to the next target on your hierarchy. One of the terrific things about this process is that as it unfolds, even before you get to the higher anxiety stimuli, their SUDS ratings decrease.

In vivo desensitization

In vivo – Latin for "in the living" -- means you actually experience exposure to the stimuli or situations you fear. Start with the least anxiety-provoking situation. After becoming deeply relaxed, approach the first situation on the hierarchy. Try to breathe abdominally throughout the exercise. Stay in the situation for several minutes; if your anxiety exceeds the 4 rating for a minute or two, either revisit your relaxation exercise and then continue or try again in your next planned desensitization session. Repeat this exposure until it no longer evokes an anxiety response. Then move on to your next target. Generally, the time for each session for both types of desensitization is 30 minutes, unless your anxiety is too great.

An example

Let's say that when you were a small child a dog jumped on you and your heart beat right out of your chest. After that, you wanted nothing to do with dogs, and your fear generalized to cats and even small creatures. Fact is, now you stay away from areas where an animal might appear -- and you're 33 years old. How do you get beyond something that has been going on for so long, is so much a part of you and has seriously restricted your choices? Answer: you commit to the process of desensitization. Your hierarchy might look like this:

Stimulus -- SUDS Rating

o Looking at a picture of a small docile dog -- 2
o Looking at a picture of a large menacing dog -- 3
o Watching a movie with a dog in a prominent role -- 4
o Observing a small dog on a leash 100 feet away -- 4
o Observing a large dog on a leash 100 feet away -- 4
o Looking out the window at a friend's dog -- 4
o Taking a walk in your neighborhood -- 5
o Visiting the pet store and petting a dog -- 6
o Going to a dog park where dogs are required to be on leashes -- 7
o Sitting in a park area where there are children, dogs and cats -- 8
o Holding a small dog for three minutes -- 8
o Letting a small, unleashed dog jump on you -- 8
o Petting a large, unleashed dog -- 9
o Letting a large dog jump on you -- 9
o Becoming a veterinarian! -- ?????

One of the first clients with whom I worked on desensitization was a five-year-old who was virtually housebound because of her fear of dogs. We actually performed most of the above steps, both in imagination and in vivo. She really did a super job. I got a call from her mother several years later to let me know that her phobia never returned. In fact, they had two large dogs now, and my little client told her teacher she wanted to be a veterinarian. Sweet!

Some additional pointers

Desensitization takes practice, practice, and more practice. You should adopt realistic expectations about how long this may take. If you're moving slowly, that's fine. Remember, you're moving and not avoiding -- that's the important part.

Some people find it helpful to record their imagery desensitization. Your relaxation exercises can also be recorded.

When starting your in vivo desensitization, you may want to have someone go with you for your initial sessions. For example, in the dog phobia, the child's mother joined us for many of the targets on the hierarchy

This procedure is quite effective, even if the items at the top of your hierarchy evoke sheer terror.

You need to come to terms with the possibility that you'll experience some discomfort. Try to normalize that idea. Discomfort is a part of life. If you tell yourself that it's awful to experience discomfort, then you leave yourself with no room to be powerful on your own behalf. Instead, tell yourself that it's just "part of the deal," and that by addressing its source, you won't let it get the best of you.

Setbacks are another part of the learning curve. Normalize those in your self-talk. Expect setbacks to happen. Your response to them should be, "Oh well!"

Be your own cheerleader in this process. Talk yourself into sticking with it. Tell yourself that this is the route to personal freedom and self-confidence. If you need help beyond what's described here, there are more extensive resources below. Also, many clinicians are well-trained to help you with this process. Best of luck!

Recommended resources

Books and recordings by Edmund Bourne, Ph.D.
The Anxiety and Phobia Workbook (2000) New Harbinger, Oakland, CA paperback

Beyond Anxiety and Phobia (2001) New Harbinger, Oakland Ca. paperback

Audiocassettes on following fears: Flying, Giving a Talk, Driving on the Highway, Heights

A final word from the author

What we believe about ourselves, others and the world in which we live makes a huge difference in our efforts to build healthy relationships and extract maximum happiness from life. It's my sincere hope that I've not only helped you understand some of the "crazy beliefs" that hold us back in these efforts, but also explained how they can be overcome using a variety of exhaustively researched, scientifically proven techniques that are the backbone of the burgeoning Positive Psychology movement. Remember: the crazy beliefs that afflict people are simply behaviors that have been *learned* over time. As such, they can be *unlearned* and replaced with effective new ways of dealing with all the curves that life throws our way.

The importance and value of the work being done in the exciting field of Positive Psychology cannot be overstated. If you'd like to learn more, please visit my website at www.PositivePathLife Coaching.com as well as www.AuthenticHappiness.com. And if you have any questions or comments, please feel free to email me at ThePositivePath@cox.net.

Sharon S. Esonis, Ph.D.
Psychologist & Life Coach